- **John Maxwell, President, The John Maxwell Company:** Bill Butterworth knows how to communicate! He brings passion and expertise to his presentations. He knows how to deliver the goods. It's my pleasure to recommend him to you.

- **Chuck Swindoll, Chancellor Emeritus, Dallas Theological Seminary:** My long-term friend and trusted colleague, Bill Butterworth has a genuine love, a desire to strengthen relationships and delightful skills in communicating. I am pleased to recommend him to you.

- **Rick Warren, Pastor, Saddleback Community Church:** It's a pleasure to recommend Bill Butterworth to you. He always delivers the goods. His humor, authenticity and love are contagious.

- **Lee Strobel, Author, *The Case for Christ:*** Bill Butterworth is one of the most captivating and effective communicators I've ever seen. I appreciate his winsome style and practical, insightful teaching.

- **Bill Hybels, Pastor, Willow Creek Community Church:** Bill Butterworth is a rare communicator. He reaches people of any age or stage in life. His warmth and humor make even the most difficult challenges easy to accept. He works his way right into your heart.

- **Craig Barnes, President, Princeton Theological Seminary:** I know of only one person better at telling parables than Bill Butterworth and that's the Savior to whom Bill is clearly devoted. This book is important, not only for its relevant content, but also as a model of effective communication.

- **Jud Wilhite, Pastor, Central Christian Church:** I appreciate Bill's style—simple, without being simplistic. To the point, but not at the expense of humor, wit and grace.

- **Rene Schlaepfer, Pastor, Twin Lakes Church:** Bill's writing is exactly the same as Bill's speaking: very funny, very smart, and very, very relevant. Bill has a way of sneaking up on you—one minute you're in hysterics over his description of a childhood faux pas, and the next minute you're realizing a life-transforming spiritual insight.

- **John Pearson, Management Consultant:** Bill Butterworth is always poignant, positive and powerful. Wit and wisdom are at it again in this very special book.

- **Gene Appel, Senior Pastor, Eastside Christian Church:** Bill Butterworth is a master communicator and humorist. Bill has lived each word of this book. You will find life in every page. He has positively influenced my life and I know he is about to influence yours as well.

- **Jamie Rasmussen, Pastor, Scottsdale Bible Church:** The trick for any great communicator is to do three things: help us understand truth, get us fired up about truth, and then help us to live out the truth. Bill Butterworth is a master of all three!

- **Walt Disney Company:** We were impressed with his presentation style, content, and his ability to connect with the audience. The response we received from our convention attendees was overwhelmingly positive. He is an outstanding communicator, versatile in his approach and content.

- **Microsoft:** Bill provided our team with "down-to-earth" solutions in dealing with the challenges of the fast paced software industry. He did it with humor and easy to remember principles that kept the group engaged throughout the session.

- **Ford Motor Company:** Your presentation was a big success! The entire management team stated how much they enjoyed it. We look forward to hearing you again.

- **American Express:** Your remarks were challenging and the audience was very responsive. In a hard charging business environment it is difficult to maintain perspective and your talk was very appropriate in this regard. We look forward to a repeat opportunity in the future.

- **Bank of America:** Judging from the audience response as well as the feedback we have heard, you hit a "Home Run!" Your mix of humor and message was just what we had hoped for.

- **Daimler Chrysler:** Thank you for making this the best meeting we've had! You were terrific. You were able to bring joy and laughter to a group of senior executives. I would recommend your presentations to any group seeking to improve morale or simply develop key member's leadership skills.

- **Young President's Organization:** Bill's presentations are dynamite! He has the rare ability to relax his audience with humor, followed by a powerful, riveting message driven home forcefully.

# Everyday

# Everyday

INFLUENCE

## Bill Butterworth

REDEMPTION
PRESS

Published by Redemption Press, PO Box 427, Enumclaw, WA 98022 Toll Free (844) 2REDEEM (273-3336)

Redemption Press is honored to present this title in partnership with the author. The views expressed or implied in this work are those of the author. Redemption Press provides our imprint seal representing design excellence, creative content and high quality production.

ISBN 13: 978-1-63232-403-0

Library of Congress Catalog Card Number: 2015938656

*To the entire Butterworth family,*
*Who influence me everyday*

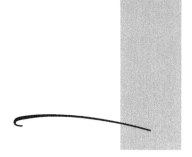

# Contents

# The Captivation of Everyday Influence

influence

in·flu·ence

ˈinflooəns

NOUN

The capacity to have an effect on the character, development, or behavior of someone or something.

\*       \*       \*

Like me, his name was Bill.

He possessed a winsome laugh, kind eyes, and a sense of humor that people found contagious. He could also wiggle his ears. But other than that, he was mostly a vanilla speck in a spumoni world.

He grew up in a row house in downtown Philadelphia in the 1920's and 1930's. As a result, he had his share of experiences being raised during the Great Depression. His brother once told me that as soon as Bill was old enough, he would run out of the red brick inner city school building every day at 3 to work at the local corner grocery store. His one indulgence was popular Big Band music and somehow he worked out a way to borrow an alto saxophone from his public school. Classes, job, homework, practice the sax—that was life in his world. Peers in his neighborhood were not expected to go on to college, and neither was Bill. The fact that he received a high school diploma was met with as much pride as a Ph.D. in today's world. In those growing up years, not much was said about not enough food to last the week, or not enough hours given his dad at his place of employment. These statements were true, but just not spoken.

Thanks to people like Cornelius Vanderbilt, Jay Gould, and Andrew Carnegie, railroads were a major, if not the major industry in the years when the unlikely influential person named Bill was growing up. But in stark contrast with Corny, Jay, and Andy, Bill's work on the railroad was at a much different level. His life's work couldn't be characterized as railroad ownership, nor was it railroad leadership, nor was it railroad management. Bill was classic blue collar, working in the freight division of the railroad whose name you know even if you don't know railroads. If you've ever played *Monopoly*, you know the Reading Railroad. Bill worked for them for 41 years. His entire family of origin was all about the railroad, from the tip of their cowcatcher to the rear platform of their caboose. His father was an electrician for the Reading, and his father-in-law was a Reading engineer, steering the mighty Iron Horse down the cold steel trails. Bill's brother and the woman who would become Bill's wife sold tickets to passengers at the Reading Terminal on Market Street, just a couple of blocks from City Hall in downtown Philadelphia.

Blue-collar work on the railroad was hard work, as seen in Bill's calloused hands. It was outdoor work, even in the dead of winter, as seen in Bill's ruddy cheeks. Like many American companies in the early 1940's, Bill was promised his job on the railroad would be held for him when he returned from his stint in the army during World War II. And they kept their promise.

When asked to describe his military service, Bill was characteristically a man of few words. "I drove a tank in North Africa," he would answer succinctly.

"Did you ever see combat?"

"No. But I did see Eisenhower once." He would laugh, give a lightning fast wink, and a wiggle of the ears.

More important than seeing Eisenhower, when Bill got back from the war, Bill saw Caroline. She sold tickets right next to Bill's brother, Joe. They met in 1950, married in 1951, and had a baby boy in 1952 and a baby girl in 1958. In myriad ways, Bill was the classic father of the Baby Boomer family. It was all about making sure the wife and kids had food to eat, clothes to wear, and a roof over their heads. There just wasn't time in the day for conversations, or long walks, or even cheering kids on at their Little League games. Other things were more important.

Bill never had much to say, but to make matters more complicated, he was diagnosed with cancer on his vocal chords when he was in his forties. The good news was they were able to cut out all the cancer. The bad news is that they took a fair amount of his vocal chords during the surgery, so for the rest of his life he would speak in a raspy sounding voice that took some getting used to and was a major source of embarrassment in his life. If he was a man of few words before the cancer, after he was just about wordless.

Bill breathed air through three-quarters of the twentieth century, from 1921 till 1996. In an odd, almost macabre statement of similarity, he died at 75, just like his father, his mother, his older sister and his younger brother. I knew him for 44 years and he was the most influential person in my life.

Bill was my father.

*       *       *

It was Thanksgiving Day 1960.

I was eight years old.

A crisp late autumn morning, I was bundled up in my winter wardrobe—plaid flannel shirt, worn cardigan sweater, dark corduroy pants, wool socks, scuffed up loafers, all topped off by a winter coat and hat with flaps to cover one's ears. In this cold weather garb, two of my three most distinguishing physical characteristics were concealed. I was overweight for my age, but it was cloaked under the ample winter coat. And I had white blonde hair, completely hidden by the hat made famous by the Russian army. All that was left as distinct was the pair of eyeglasses, jet-black frames, and magnified lenses. Clark Kent meets Mr. Magoo.

"Your father works on Thanksgiving so he can have Christmas day off," my mom explained to me, as she double-checked to see if my sweater was buttoned and my jacket zipped. It would have been unthinkable to get that much verbiage out of Dad. "The railroad runs every day of the year, so we are thankful he has enough seniority to get December 25th off."

I nodded in silent agreement, but in my mind there was a bigger story than Dad having to work on Thanksgiving.

Dad has invited me *to go to work with him* on this Thanksgiving holiday.

Most of his coworkers have the day off, so it will be a quieter version of a day on the railroad. I can't honestly explain the motivation behind my father inviting me. I want to say that it was because he wanted some quality time with his only son. But it would be much more likely that Dad was told to babysit the boy by my Mom so she could get all the extra tasks accomplished for our extended family Thanksgiving dinner set for that afternoon with all the uncles, aunts, cousins, and grandparents arriving at our house about the same time the railroad men would be heading home.

I said good-bye to my mother and wandered out the back door from which my dad had already departed. He was in our car, a 1957 Ford Fairlane 500, already warming it up for our drive from the suburbs to the downtown riverbank. Excitedly hopping into the front passenger seat, I was surprised to hear my Dad actually make a comment. "Your mother and I listen to WFIL on the radio." (This was a fact I already knew since it was where the radio was set at the house as well—*560 on the dial, relax awhile with WFIL. Philadelphia. WFIL*—as the jingle went.)

"I listen to Uncle Philsy on the way to work and then I listen to Wee Willie Webber on the way home." Radio was different back then. Today it seems like your options are all-talk as in Talk Radio, or all music, as in a Top 40 station where a voice only interrupts every twenty minutes with the call letters of the station. In 1960 Uncle Philsy and Wee Willie Webber were disc jockeys—guys who played records over the radio and interspersed between songs witty banter, charming conversation, and grand entertainment of their own. It only took a few minutes for me to decode what I just heard from my father—there will be no conversations in the car. But just sitting next to him in the front seat was exhilarating. I was doing life with him. I was content with my car-mates, Frank Sinatra and Nat 'King' Cole—and of course, Uncle Philsy.

It's okay. I am about to spend the day with my father at his place of employment—an address of intrigue that I had heard only bits and pieces about over the years. It's the freight office—the place where Dad and all his railroad buddies would congregate early in the morning and at the end of each workday to swap war stories, both literally and figuratively. Dad had recently been promoted from Car Inspector to Chief Car Inspector, and the additional responsibilities could be summarized in three words—*more paper work*. So this office had become a new home for my father, although the use of the word 'home' is quite generous, to be sure.

"Follow me, Pal," Dad instructed. (He never called me 'Son'—it was always 'Pal'). He added, "And stay close." We climbed a flight of rickety stairs in an old, two-story office building made of red brick, faded of course, after many years of existence. At the top of the stairs, we turned right and walked into the office. It was a compact room with only enough square footage for a large wooden desk in the center and a smaller desk off to the side in a corner. The window shades were drawn shut and it was obvious that even on pretty days, one wouldn't want to open the windows to enjoy the breeze. The smell of the mighty Delaware in those days would end that option immediately. The office was cold, with a temperamental heater, so it would be a little bit of time before I shed the winter coat in favor of just the sweater.

Granted, it was Thanksgiving, but take all the warmth and love and joy that was waiting in that suburban dining room setting back home and replace it with an office reflecting years of neglect. Desks, chairs, and office supplies made it look 25 years older than it really was. Dust was everywhere. Even dirt and grime in certain spots. Echoes of familial love and joy were replaced by the solitary sound of a wall clock, working away the seconds with its ceaseless passing of the pendulum. Even though no one had occupied the office for the last twelve hours, it still had the distinct smell of cigar smoke and if there was any doubt, there was a gray haze that floated at ceiling level to overarch and underscore the fact. My dad didn't smoke so this fragrance was a whole new notion for my nostrils. It was 1960, but this run down building in the Port Richmond section of Philadelphia felt like a locale right out of a Dickens novel a century before with the only addition being electricity.

It was to be just the two of us for the entire office visit. As if he forgot that I came along with him, Dad immediately took his place at the large desk, sighed a sigh and began addressing the mountain of forms that arose from his worn, faded desk blotter. I stood silently, watching him work, wondering if this was going to be how the day unfolded—Dad working at the big desk, me standing by silently in a bit of a confused state.

That's when he looked up and smiled at me. Silently, he pointed his finger towards the smaller desk in the corner, as if I should understand what a pointing finger meant. I turned my attention to a wooden desk only big enough to have drawers going down each side and an opening in the middle for an adult to place two legs when sitting at it. A cold metal lamp sat to the left, a fixture that looked old enough to have come from Edison's personal collection. A tin can of sorts was placed on the right side, filled with pencils, brown in color and each one stamped in gold with the words *READING COMPANY No. 2*. But it was the machine in the middle of the desktop that took my breath away.

The centerpiece of the small desk was the large contraption placed upon it. I had seen these machines on television, but this was my first opportunity to see one in person. Almost cubical in shape, it was a mass of metal that featured four rows of keys the size of pennies, each with a different letter, number, or symbol emblazoned upon it. It was black, with the exception of nine letters and a royal crest that unfolded along the back strip of black metal. *Underwood* it read and I was enthralled to get my first look at a typewriter.

Dad led me over to the small desk, pulled out the equally small chair and with that gesture, he silently invited me to sit down. Once in the chair, he leaned over me to insert a single piece of paper into the typewriter, getting it into position to begin typing. Boy in chair, paper in typewriter, all systems were 'go.' With that preamble in place, my dad uttered four words.

"*You might like this.......*"he almost whispered in his soft, raspy tone.

And with that teaser, he silently returned to his desk, eight feet away, and began pouring over a pile of paperwork that had multiplied over the weeks of neglect due to weightier matters out in the railroad yard.

Without the need of any coaxing, I began pecking away at the typewriter keys, each peck sounding like a small firecracker exploding illegally in the backyard on the Fourth of July. Strong, bold black letters began to appear on the white paper, most in perfect order, but a few, like the small letter 'a', would land a little higher on the line than the other letters, giving it a place of unique distinction. My first order of business was to record how fun this typewriting really was:

*I am with Daddy at work.*
*I am typing on a typewriter.*
*I am having a really good time.*

Soon that staccato pop would create a beautifully descriptive set of sentences, being reproduced on multiple sheets of paper, except these copies were in letter form.

*Dear Mommy,*
  *I am with Daddy at work.*
  *I am typing on a typewriter.*
  *I am having a really good time.*
      *Love, Billy*

This went on for hours. Letters were typed to all the aunts, uncles, grandparents and cousins that we would be seeing later that afternoon at Thanksgiving dinner. Extra epistles were reproduced to all my friends in the neighborhood. As I was working through the thirty names of the kids in my third grade class, Dad interrupted my publishing endeavors with the sudden pronouncement, "Okay, Pal, it's time to go home."

Where had the time gone? I was captivated by the whole experience. I had become so enamored by the unbelievable Underwood that the entire day was spent sitting before it, pecking away, one index finger from each hand, chronicling my adventure as if I had just scaled Kilimanjaro or won the Nobel Peace Prize.

We had even worked through lunch, a major accomplishment for a boy who did all his clothes shopping in the department marked 'husky.'

In that slice of office time, in that musty smelling room with the settled dust and the sound of the pendulum, I had discovered something more than a typewriter. I had discovered writing. Today, I sit in front of the Underwood's great-great-great grandchild and peck away at the craft I have come to adore.

Perhaps my life would have gone differently if my dad had not invited me to go to work with him that Thanksgiving of 1960. Even though in retrospect, it appears to be the most mundane of conversations, seemingly without any deep meaning whatsoever, I know differently. That was the day my passion for writing was fueled. There was a lasting impact resulting from four simple syllables.

*"You might like this . . . ."*

**Influence arrives in the simplest of ways.**

# CHAPTER 1

# The Calling of Everyday Influence

calling

call·ing

ˈkôliNG

NOUN

A strong urge toward a particular way of life or career; a vocation: *those who have a special calling to minister to others' needs.*

\*     \*     \*

Izzy was Laurel to Bart's Hardy.

A veritable wisp of a man, Izzy couldn't have been over five feet tall and he certainly didn't weigh more than one hundred pounds. Age had not been kind to this gentle little man in his early sixties, as evidenced by the gray hair and the myriad wrinkles displayed on any uncovered area of skin. As much as he tried to walk erect, his shoulders drooped and he had the slightest hint of a hunch on his back. His eyesight was failing, necessitating the thick lens surrounded by the large black frames.

Every day I spent with him, he wore the identical outfit; a plain white t-shirt, brown slacks, brown socks and brown shoes that looked more like slippers than any other shoe style. I don't think it was the same shirt and pants every day, but then again, I cannot be certain.

Without question, the most distinguishing characteristic of my friend Izzy was between his nose and his chin. Izzy's mouth was so attention getting for the simple reason that Izzy had no teeth. To be more precise, he had teeth, but he chose to keep them wrapped in a piece of wax paper, safely tucked in the right front pocket of his brown slacks. Besides eating, he made it clear that the teeth were only to be used for special occasions. As many people do who have no teeth, Izzy had a nervous habit of always giving the impression he was chewing on something. It was quite the juxtaposition to observe this tiny man appearing to be constantly eating. Dear sweet Izzy couldn't have taken in more than seven hundred calories on any given day.

On the opposite end of the food chain was Bart. This man could take in seven hundred calories in a matter of minutes. Stated in the simplest of terms, Bart was the biggest man I had ever met up to that point in my life. To say he was enormous is like saying Michael Jordan had a good run with the round ball. I never had the courage to ask him how much he weighed but I would guess he was near four hundred pounds. He was in his early fifties, with a wave of brown hair that he combed straight back along with a hair product that kept it in place. Piercing green eyes and a kind smile, Bart had one of those faces where the chin had disappeared. Instead of a little bit of a jut protruding from the bottom of his head, like most of us with a chin, Bart's extra weight caused his face to drop down to his body in a straight line. It looked like a sculptor had chiseled out the head, but never bothered finishing the project as the face grew out of an untouched block of marble.

Like Izzy, Bart wore the same thing every day; plain white t-shirt, slacks, socks and shoes. Unlike Izzy, the slacks were blue and the shoes were more like loafers. Also unlike Izzy, Bart had teeth. Most of them, anyway. When he smiled there was a gap or two that became apparent, but there was really nothing about Bart's face that was all that noteworthy.

It was his body that was noteworthy. That massive trunk that was attached to two relatively short skinny legs would make even the most polite person do a double take. His stomach would hang over his trousers to such a degree that it looked like Bart was carrying triplets. The t-shirt did little to disguise what was going on. It was the sort of appearance my dear mother used to describe as 'a beer belly.'

She had no idea how right she was.

Bart, by his own admission, lived each day for five-o-clock. Punch his time card, get in his truck and cruise down the street to the closest bar. An unmarried man, Bart would spend his entire evening sitting on that metal bar stool with the red vinyl seat. If barstools could talk, that red one would have moaned in pain under the massive weight of his favorite customer. Somehow Bart would get himself home, crash into bed and manage to make it to work the next morning in time to punch in at 8 A.M.

"What do you do all night at that bar?" I once asked him.

"Drink beer," was the two-word reply. Then he would add, "Busch beer." He had a unique way of pronouncing the word 'Busch' for it always came out sounding like 'Booosh' as he elongated the sound of the 'ooo's.

I'm not sure how much Bart would eat, but I could tell you without fear of contradiction that he could drink more beer than the average three guys combined. Most likely it was his extra tonnage that allowed him to drink as much as he did without the corresponding consequences of falling face first on the floor blind stinking drunk.

Which brings us back to Izzy.

These two men, Bart and Izzy, worked together at the same factory in their hometown of Miami, Florida. Bart was the foreman in a department that included only two other workers. One worker was Izzy. The other worker was me. Every Monday through Friday the three of us would stand at our machines doing our work (I'll explain our work and the machines as the story continues to develop). I manned the middle machine, with Bart to my right and Izzy to my left. The two of them would converse with each other as if I didn't even exist. I was a college student at the time, so there was a huge age gap that the two of them didn't want to attempt to close with conversation. But to make it even worse, I was a *Bible College* student and Bart found that fact to be especially offensive, since he concluded I was looking down on him and judging him for his lust for massive quantities of alcoholic beverage. This was not the truth whatsoever, but it was the way Bart saw it and I had to live with it.

Another part of the reason Bart would converse with Izzy right over my head was due to the nature of the conversation. Every dialog, for just about every day I worked there, could be summarized in one key invitation:

"Izzy," Bart would shout over the noise of the machine, "you need to come drinking with me tonight. You need to drink some Booosh."

Izzy's response was always the same. "Not tonight, Bart," he would say while gumming his invisible food.

This conversation went on for days, weeks, and months, until the fateful day Izzy said yes to Bart's daily invitation.

I don't know why Izzy said yes, just like I don't know why he had refused up to this point. Yes, Izzy was a kind man, but I would not go so far as to say he was a man of strong character or self-discipline. If I had to guess, I would surmise that Izzy didn't go drinking because he felt like he didn't have the money for it. We were all working hourly labor at minimum wage, so no one was getting rich at this job. But for some unexplained reason Izzy relented and joined Bart at the bar for a few beers.

It goes without saying that the innocent, young and naïve Bible College student did not join these two. I wasn't even invited. But I did observe what happened the next morning and it was quite evident that what had taken place the night before was having an impact on the morning after.

Apparently Izzy not only accompanied Bart to the bar, but he also tried to keep up with him by drinking as much beer as Bart downed. Are you doing the math? A one hundred-pounder sitting next to a four hundred pounder pounding down the brews. Izzy was three sheets to the wind in no time.

Bart got Izzy home without any damage, but Izzy's behavior at work the following morning was not as simple.

Let me tell you a little bit about our work at this factory so you'll fully appreciate Izzy's fall from grace.

The three of us worked in a factory that made wallets. Not rich leather wallets, but plastic, vinyl wallets. The kind of wallets that are sold at tourist traps as souvenirs, especially if they are gold stamped with the logo of the tourist attraction. This was all taking place in the early 1970's in Miami. Walt Disney World was still a year or two away, so the smaller attractions in Miami were still drawing crowds. People flocked to *Parrot Jungle* to see the birds of many colors perform tricks and sit on your shoulder for your photo to be taken. Tourists still lined up to visit *Monkey Jungle* where you could see chimpanzees participate in shows that would get you laughing so hard, you'd be in tears. And of course, it was also before *Sea World* so a visit to the *Seaquarium* would entertain you with whales, sharks and those adorable Miami dolphins.

All these places needed souvenir wallets and that's where our factory came to the rescue. Large rolls of vinyl would be cut into rectangular pieces, which in turn would be heat-sealed together to create the wallet itself. The wallet was then taken to the gold stamper for the all-important logo of a bird, a monkey, or a fish.

Bart, Izzy and I accomplished step one—the cutting of the vinyl from the large rolls into the small rectangles. To do this, each of us stood at the end of a long, narrow wooden table. Each one of them was about five feet wide and about twenty feet long. We would place the roll of vinyl at the far end of the table and roll out a piece that was twenty feet long. With a box cutter, we would slice the vinyl free from the roll. Then we would repeat that process, placing another twenty-foot piece of vinyl on top of the previous one, cutting it as well. We would do this twenty times, so that the end product was a stretch of vinyl twenty feet long, five feet wide and twenty pieces deep. We'd staple the sheets together on the two outside edges and we were ready for the next step.

At our end of the long narrow table was a large machine. Made of steel, the central feature was a huge steel plate that hung about a foot above the table. Above the plate were two red buttons, about eighteen inches apart, perfectly set, one for your right hand and the other for your left. Using a finger from both of your hands, by pressing the red buttons the large steel plate would crash downward towards the stack of vinyl.

One more piece of equipment was necessary to finalize this process. It's called a die and ours was made from a one inch thick piece of wood, cut into the shape of the potential wallet. Surrounding the outer edge of the die was a strip of metal, about two inches high. This meant that an inch of the steel was exposed around the wood and that inch was sharpened so that upon the steel crash, it would cut the vinyl into the desired shape.

The three of us would each place our die on the vinyl, press the buttons, make the cut, remove the cut vinyl into a pile to our right and them move the die into position to do it again. And again. And again. Until all twenty feet of vinyl was cut up. And then we'd roll out another twenty layers and do it all over again. It was pretty mundane work without the possibility of much that could happen to mess it up.

Until the day Izzy came to work hung over.

The morning after his 'Booosh-athon' with Bart, Izzy came to work in a world of hurt. His usually quiet demeanor was interrupted by constant moans and groans, indicative of a guy with a major headache. After he punched in, he went about his normal routine, which began by unfolding the twenty layers of vinyl onto his long narrow workstation.

It was what happened next that had the lasting impact on the situation. Poor Izzy, head pounding, muscles aching, eyes blurred and focus distorted placed the die on the vinyl for the first cut of the day. In the pain of the moment, Izzy placed the die on the stack of vinyl, unaware that the die was *upside down*. Fingers on the red buttons, he pounded that die into the vinyl, only to discover that no cuts had been made. Instead, the die had been smashed, corrupted, contorted and distorted. The sharp edges of the blade, previously in the shape of a rectangle were now in a tangled web of asymmetry.

Immediately aware of his mistake, Izzy turned the die over to the position it was supposed to maintain during the cutting process. He placed his fingers on the red buttons, pressed them and cut the twenty sheets of vinyl. But the die, in its mangled condition was no longer cutting perfect rectangles. It was cutting the vinyl into shapes that looked like Picasso on drugs.

It became immediately apparent that it wasn't just the die that was messed up. The die was impacting the twenty sheets of vinyl. The die's shape, or in this case misshape, became the vinyl's ultimate condition. There was no escaping it. The die was impacting and influencing the vinyl beneath it.

Izzy appeared dazed and confused as he watched the misshapen sheets of vinyl stack up. It didn't take long before Bart observed what was happening and the scolding began. "Izzy, you @#$%!" Bart screamed. "What did you do to the die? You're making a mess out of everything!" There's no doubt Izzy was sorry for what had happened, but the damage had already been done. The vinyl had been irreparably impacted by the irregular die.

Izzy, Bart and I will never forget the events of that fateful day. And by the way, something else occurred that day.....

....It was Izzy's first day as the factory's janitor.

*　　*　　*

We are *all* called to influence.

If you are breathing, you have influence. If you've got a pulse, you've got impact. It doesn't matter if you're big like Bart or small like Izzy. You can be in perfect shape like the die before being smashed by Izzy or you can be as out of shape as an upside down die that collided with a steel plate. It doesn't matter. All of us have significant influence in the lives of all the people with whom we have contact.

We all influence others just like the die influences the vinyl. This symbol is not original with me. Others have used it, but of most interest to me is how it is used in the Bible's New Testament. My first exposure to this concept was when I read Peter's words to his fellow church leaders:

*Therefore, I exhort the elders among you, as your fellow elder and witness of the sufferings of Christ, and a partaker also of the glory that is to be revealed, shepherd the flock of God among you, exercising oversight not under compulsion, but voluntarily, according to the will of God; and not for sordid gain, but with eagerness; nor yet as lording it over those allotted to your charge, but proving to be **examples** to the flock.*

—1 Peter 5:1-3 NASB (emphasis added)

It's that word 'examples' that caught my attention. The Greek word is 'tupon' (rhymes with 'coupon') and it means 'the mark of a blow, or a stamp struck by a die.' Peter is encouraging individuals to stamp your life on the life of others, as a die would impact a pile of vinyl. Or like the keys of an Underwood Manual Typewriter strike the white paper with the blackness of the ink. It's the same word that our friend Doubting Thomas uses after Christ's resurrection when he says:

*So the other disciples were saying to him, "We have seen the Lord!" But he said to them, "Unless I see in His hands the **imprint** of the nails, and put my finger into the place of the nails, and put my hand into His side, I will not believe."*

—John 20:25 NASB (emphasis added)

In effect Thomas says, "Unless I can see the impression left by the nails, the impact, the influence those nails made on His body, I will not believe." That's 'tupon.'

Paul uses 'tupon' in his encouragement to the Thessalonians:

*So that you became an **example** to all the believers in Macedonia and in Achaia.*

—First Thessalonians 1:7 NASB (emphasis added)

"Your life has been impacting others," Paul says, "So I am pleased that it's been a positive impact."

'Tupon.' We've all got it, so we might as well use it for good. Perhaps a helpful way to view our influence is to view it as part of our calling.

The Oxford Dictionary defines 'calling' as 'a strong urge towards a particular way of life.' We tend to think of calling as something out of the ordinary, like a person's call to ministry. But, I want you to think of the concept of calling in a much broader context.

We are *all* called to influence because, as human beings, we are all constantly impacting those around us. Sometimes our influence is good, sometimes it is bad. Influence is rarely neutral. Sometimes the influence is in big chunks, but most times the influence is in small, bite-size tidbits, and therein lays the secret sauce for greater influential effectiveness.

Most everything I've ever read on the subject of influence tends to focus on the big chunks. The small tidbits are sometimes included, but almost as an afterthought. But think about the people who influenced your life. Didn't a great deal of that influence occur through a casual statement in the midst of a conversation? Or maybe it was something small that they did for you, like point you towards a typewriter in the hopes that you might like it.

It was the artist Andy Warhol who made popular the concept that each of us will get our fifteen minutes of fame. That's a fascinating concept, but it's simply not true. The truth is that most of us won't even get fifteen minutes. And that's why the concept of smaller sips of influence is more far-reaching than the big gulp.

So this book is for the CEO of a *Fortune 500* company, but it's also for the front line, minimum wage worker as well. This is for the Super

Bowl MVP and the guy who got cut from the seventh grade team. It's for the virtuoso playing Carnegie Hall, and the woman who gave it her best shot, but came to the conclusion the cello was not her cup of tea. It's for your state's Governor, and the person who lost a close election for tenth grade president. It's not about a role. It's about a God-given life.

It's for everybody who has not yet flat-lined.

Small stuff screams significance.

Influence is for everyone.

You have it, whether you realize it or not.

**Influence includes all of us.**

# CHAPTER 2

# The Commencement of Everyday Influence

commencement

com·mence·ment

*kuh*-mens-m*uh* nt

NOUN

The act or celebration of beginning.

\*       \*       \*

Less than a year after my Thanksgiving introduction to the Underwood Manual Typewriter, my world was rocked with the force of a tsunami.

We moved.

For nine years I had been digging my roots into the suburban Philadelphia soil of a small town named Ambler. Our little house on 231 Overlook Road was perfect, as far as I was concerned. Sure it was small—only two bedrooms and one bath, so when my sister came along in 1958 my parents had to get creative. Their solution was to finish off the unfinished attic in this early version of a tract house. The finished attic ended up being two large rooms. One was to be used as a bedroom; the other was to be a playroom. And they were both all for me. So while Dad was at work and my mom and sister lived their lives on the home's main floor, the attic was my kingdom, which suited my vivid imagination just fine. One day the attic would be the locker room at Connie Mack Stadium, home of the Philadelphia Phillies, where I would chat it up with some of my favorite players from the late 50's and early 60's. Another day it would be the bunkhouse at the ranch shared with Spin and Marty, two fictional characters I followed closely on the *Mickey Mouse Club*. Most days it was my pretend office, where I would work at my real desk, answering the pretend phone, while pounding away at my pretend typewriter.

When I needed a change of environment, I would hustle down the steps, slip out the back door and stroll across Overlook Road to adjoining Artman Road to the home of my best friend, Billy Holmes. I'd usually have my old baseball glove, or a small stack of baseball cards with me, so that we were certain to have something to do. Billy lived across the street from a large house that the local Catholic Church owned and operated as a home for seniors. It too, was on Artman Road and it was creatively named Artman Home. The best part of that place was the large field that was adjacent to the back of the house. My friend Billy, an altar boy and member in good standing of St. Anthony's Catholic Church, would know exactly how to sweet talk the nuns into letting us use the field as a baseball diamond. My friend had a way with the Sisters! (He had me convinced that as a young Presbyterian, I would never understand how to make nice with a nun.)

We spent hours on that field, playing baseball, pretending we were the real Philadelphia Phillies, who were so bad back then that we were totally convinced that a couple of elementary school kids could bolster their lineup and make them actual contenders for the National League pennant.

We even played ball on rainy days. The only exceptions were the days when it was beyond rainy—those stormy days where you couldn't see the ball when it was pitched to you. On those days we would hang out in Billy's garage with our baseball card collections. I always had a stack with me, tucked into the back pocket of my faded blue jeans. But if we knew we were going to play with the cards for an extended period of time, I would bring my entire collection. We all kept our cards in the same kind of box—a used cigar box. The dimensions of the box were perfect for two long stacks of cards, running side by side along the interior. And of course, the cigar brand of choice was *Phillies*. Even to this day, I have an empty old *Phillies* cigar box on a shelf in my office, because just looking at it takes me back to a time of delightfully peaceful innocence. (Notice I said 'empty' cigar box. Like so many of my fellow Baby Boomers, our mothers threw away all our baseball cards when we went off to college. What was wrong with these mothers, that they didn't have the sense to know what was really important in life?)

There were two elementary schools in Ambler, one was located on Mattison Avenue and held Kindergarten through second grade and the other, found on Forrest Avenue housed third grade through sixth. In keeping with the days of creative titling, the schools were named Mattison Avenue School and Forrest Avenue School. Both buildings were large, two-story, imposing structures made of solid gray stone that, to today's eye, would look less like a school and more like Juvenile Hall.

In my mind, I thought myself to be an average child since I was a little smarter than my peers in the mental department and a little slower than my peers physically, thanks to my extra weight. In my mind it made perfect sense—the two averaged out to make me average.

The year I was in third grade was a year of upheaval in our family, although my parents did an excellent job of shielding me from the trauma. Two of my grandparents died that year; my father's mother and my mother's father. My dad's father had passed away when I was only one year old, so I was down to one last grandparent; my mom's mom, Grandmom Rosenbaum.

Upon the death of Granddad Rosenbaum, my mother expressed her desire to have her mom move in with us. "She's all by herself now," Mom reasoned with my Dad, as I eavesdropped on the conversation from my hiding place in the back hallway. "Who will look out for her? What if she fell down the stairs? Who would even know she was hurt?" My Dad agreed with Mom's concern but both had to admit, our little Ambler house was not going to be big enough for one more occupant. It was shortly after these kinds of conversations that my grandmother approached my parents with an offer to consider: "I have a little money saved up," she began. "What if you move your family to a bigger house— like a four bedroom house and I will make up the difference for what it would cost between a three bedroom and a four bedroom? Then I will move into that fourth bedroom. Do you think that will work?"

And that's how we moved from Ambler to Southampton.

Mom and Dad found this new development of homes being built in Southampton, a town in lower Bucks County, not too far from the Philadelphia county line. The development was called Burgundy Hills and it was classic 1960's Americana Cookie Cutter Homes. With the extra money my grandmother kicked in, my parents were able to swing a two story Colonial, four bedroom, two and a half bath beauty with a two-car garage and a full basement. All for $18,490. Everyone was ecstatic.

Except me.

Leaving Ambler was not my idea of a good move. Billy Holmes wasn't moving with me, so what was I going to do for a best friend? I didn't see any Southampton version of Artman Home, so where was I going to play baseball every day? I started fourth grade not knowing anyone in my class and immediately felt less than average. I was the fat kid on the outside looking in.

The local elementary school was a sleek, one story, brick structure that was much newer and more contemporary than anything I had ever seen in Ambler. Located on Maple Avenue, I was immediately thrown by the fact that it was not called Maple Avenue School. Rather, it was named William W. H. Davis Elementary School. To this day I am not sure who William Davis was, but from that day until High School graduation, all my schooling with one grade exception would be done in buildings named after people, not streets.

Fourth grade was a real adjustment time for little Billy Butterworth. This is usually the point in the story when you start to hear about how cruel children can be to one another, and I'm afraid I have no exceptions to present to you. What the kids in Ambler seemed to accept, the kids in Southampton initially rejected with harsh criticism. Being a little smarter than the others brought teasing from my classmates. It didn't help that I was wearing even thicker lens in my glasses that year, so the taunting about the smart kid in the glasses was a prehistoric reference to what would later be called a Geek or a Nerd.

But it was my extra weight that was the killer. I was not little Billy Butterworth. I was Butterball. The kids composed their own jingle to introduce me to others:

*I see Billy Butterworth.*
*He's the fattest kid on earth.*

The deepest cut occurred on the playground. When it was recess or after school, it was time to play football or baseball or dodge ball, which meant teams needed to be chosen. The two most popular boys in the class would always be the captains and the choosing was a fairly repetitive operation. The same boys were chosen first each time. The same boys were chosen second each time. And so on, until we come to the final repetitive operation…

…. I was chosen *last* each time.

It went down that way just about every time I can remember. There was one exception that does come to mind—the time we were playing tackle football after school one crisp autumn afternoon. One of the captains announced, "I'm gonna pick Butterball now, rather than last, because we're short on guys and he can play the whole offensive line all by himself." They all laughed at me and sure enough, I played the O-line alone that day.

But there was a part of fourth grade that was as exhilarating as the playground was defeating. Twice a week, on Tuesdays and Thursdays, we would have a visitor enter our classroom for a forty-five minute diversion from math and science and social studies. Our teacher, Mrs. Forde, would welcome our guest and then dismiss herself to the Faculty Lounge for a well-deserved cup of coffee and a cigarette.

Our guest was our Music Teacher. "Hello, boys and girls," he announced excitedly. "My name is Mr. Cassell and I will be leading us in songs that we'll be singing together."

We were all stunned the first time Warren Cassell appeared in our classroom. First of all, none of us had ever been taught by a man up to that point. All our teachers had been women, so this was a groundbreaking moment indeed. Secondly, there were no musical instruments in our classroom, which meant Mr. Cassell had to bring them with him. He brought only one. A piano. This tall, slender man, impeccably dressed in a dark business suit, crisp white shirt and conservative necktie had an old brown upright piano put on large wheels so he could roll it down the hall, going from classroom to classroom in his daily journeys through the corridors of Davis Elementary.

We always began with the same song. Piano rolled into our room, Mrs. Forde safely retired to the Faculty Lounge, to the tune of *Roll Out the Barrel*, we would heartily sing:

> *Roll out the piano; we will have fun as we play,*
> *Roll out the piano, for Mrs. Forde's fourth grade today!*

Mr. Cassell fascinated me. He had one of those smiles that made his eyes disappear. His pursed lips seemed to always be chapped. But his love of music was unmistakable and for many of us it was quite contagious.

If a student truly enjoyed those two 45 minute sessions during the school day, there was an option for an after school activity that would enlarge on the musical fun. It was the Chorus. Technically it was open to any student who wanted to sign up, but not feeling all that accepted in life at that point, I figured it would be just one more joke at my expense—something like everyone can join except for Butterball.

That's why the little conversation that took place between Mr. Cassell and me one day was a game changer.

As our music class was coming to a close, Mr. Cassell always chose one student to help him roll his piano out of the room and into the next. Frankly, he could handle the piano just fine by himself, but this need for a helper gave him some one-on-one time with students in whom he saw potential.

"Billy Butterworth, will you help me roll my piano to the next classroom today?" Mr. Cassell asked.

Having never had that honor before, I eagerly jumped up from my chair and assisted him and his piano out of the classroom and into the hall.

"Billy, you look like you really enjoy singing with me in class," Mr. Cassell began.

"I do," I answered. "I like it."

"Well, you know we have the school Chorus that meets after school on Thursdays," he continued. "I think you would really love some of the songs we are singing. And we do a big concert for the whole school and all the parents every Christmas and every spring."

He paused for a moment, then added, "I think you'd fit in great in my Chorus."

I smiled and then he said the four magic words the displaced fourth grader was dying to hear:

*"Will you join me?"*

It was like the moment where Lassie and little Timmy are reunited at the end of each episode. I nodded to Mr. Cassell and with that brief interchange I became a part of the Davis Elementary School Chorus.

I thrived under Mr. Cassell's kindness towards me. The Chorus could feel as much like home as the classroom sometimes felt like a foreign desert. Mr. Cassell seemed to pick up on how important those after school sessions were becoming, so he took me aside only a few weeks after I had joined to ask a favor of me.

"Billy, do you see how all the chairs are set up in the room we sing in? I have to rearrange those chairs before and after every rehearsal. And we always have our music placed on our chairs so we're ready to sing. I have to put out all that music and then collect it when we're through. You seem to be enjoying Chorus so much I want to ask you a question:

*"Will you help me?"*

I felt so special that of all the kids in the Chorus, he wanted help from *me*. Sure, it was only lining up chairs and passing out music, but it made me feel of value. It made me feel important.

My fourth grade year in Chorus was a wonderful experience for me. As much as I was looking forward to fifth and sixth grade with Mr. Cassell, as fourth grade was winding down, I was sent home with a note one afternoon that would alter my future.

*Dear Mr. and Mrs. Butterworth:*

*Billy has shown real progress this year and I am very pleased with his academic ability. For that reason I would like to recommend Billy for the Gifted Program. With your permission he will begin it next year. Please consider this recommendation and respond with your decision.*

*Sincerely,*
*Mrs. Forde*

The Gifted Program? Are you kidding me? How ironic that I felt so displaced that year, yet my teacher thought I should go into an accelerated program. My parents decided it was the right move so I joined another set of new classmates the next fall. Most unfortunate in this decision was the collateral damage. It required me to change schools. I left Davis, which meant I had to leave Mr. Cassell and his Chorus.

As we were preparing for the Spring Concert that fourth grade year, Mr. Cassell came through for me one more time. "We're going to do a song that has a special part of the song for a boy's trio. We need three boys to sing these parts. I've looked over our guys and I'm going to ask these three boys to take the parts: Bobby Newman, Andy Tyson, and Billy Butterworth. So I have a question for you three:

*Will you sing for me?"*

Of course, we were all so flattered to be asked, we all willingly agreed in an instant. It was his way of telling us we were good; that we had potential with the gifts we possessed and we believed him.

I've never forgotten Mr. Cassell. And I'll always be grateful for his influence in my life.

\*     \*     \*

It was almost twenty years later that I heard a lecture while in Seminary that put together theology, psychology, influence and fourth grade. The professor was speaking on the topic of 'self-esteem' and he was using a book by one of the alumni as his primary reference. The book was titled *The Sensation of Being Somebody* and the author was Dr. Maurice Wagner.[1]

As human beings, we all have three great needs, the professor explained. We want to belong. We want to feel worthy. We want to be competent. Through our relationship with God, more specifically with God the Trinity, all three of these needs are met.

We want to belong. Who wouldn't want to join the family of God and have God Himself as your heavenly Father? Because of our relationship with the Father, our belongingness need is met. The Apostle John said it this way:

---

[1] Maurice Wagner, *The Sensation of Being Somebody.* (Grand Rapids, MI: Zondervan Publishers, 1975).

*But as many as received Him, to them He gave the right to become children of God, even to those who believe in His name.*

—John 1: 12 NASB

By faith, I am God's child and He is my Father. That's some pretty serious belonging.

We want to have worth. An object is worth the price paid for it. Consider the words of the Apostle Paul:

*He [God the Father] made Him [Jesus Christ, God the Son] who knew no sin to be sin on our behalf, so that we might become the righteousness of God in Him.*

—II Corinthians 5: 21 NASB

Jesus, God the Son, gave His very life for you. Does that not bolster your worth? You have value, great value.

We want to be competent. Because of our relationship with God the Spirit, each of us has been supernaturally given gifts to serve others. Once again the Apostle Paul clarifies this truth to the Corinthians:

*Now there are varieties of gifts, but the same Spirit. But to each one is given the manifestation of the Spirit for the common good.*

—I Corinthians 12: 4, 7 NASB

That means there is something within you, given to you by the Holy Spirit, that you do well. Hopefully you have discovered it by now, but even if you haven't the fact remains you are competent because of your relationship to the Holy Spirit.

In that fourth grade academic year, Mr. Cassell lived out in human terms what God does daily for us in supernatural terms. He invited me to join the Chorus, thus meeting a belongingness need. He asked me to help him before and after rehearsal, signifying to me that I was of value. And he chose me to sing in the boy's trio, showing me he believed I had musical talent.

We're not always so fortunate to have a fellow human being who can meet those kinds of needs in our life. Mr. Cassell was rare indeed. But thank God we have God—Father, Son and Holy Spirit. In Him we've got all the bases covered.

Belongingness—I'm part of;

Worth—I count;

Competence—I can.

That little triad of thoughts has been like a rock for me since I struggled with my share of insecurities, like most of us have. Whenever I have the opportunity to make a presentation that would be aided by some thoughts on self-image or self-esteem, I never fail to present that outline, of course crediting Dr. Wagner.

Years ago, I was making one such presentation in the Mount Hermon Conference Center, one of my favorite places to work. I offered my personal opinion on how valuable that tiny trio of thoughts became to me in my own life and how grateful I was to this man I had never met, for authoring this book that I found so helpful.

When the meeting concluded, a few people stayed around to thank me for my remarks, which is such a nice gesture on their part. After all were gone but one, a kind older gentleman with hair as white as snow and a smile as warm as the sun stepped forward, held out his right hand and introduced himself. "Hello, Bill. I'm Maurice Wagner. I just wanted to thank you for the very kind words you had for my writing. I appreciate it very much. I'm glad it had a positive impact on your life." I was so taken by the fact that I had been so strongly influenced decades ago by a man I had only met in person that evening.

Commencement is defined as 'the act or celebration of beginning.' We begin influence by accepting that our life will be of influence, whether we're aware of it or not. We can't fully grasp how influential our life can be in the positive sense until we have made peace with ourselves concerning who we are. And we can't make peace with ourselves until we have made peace with God. By accepting the Lord Jesus, we begin an eternal relationship that will always have as its foundation the meeting of our most significant needs.

Influence begins by accepting yourself the way God made you. You belong to Him. You have worth because of Him. You have competency because you are related to Him. Once you have that down, you are ready to become a positive influence in the lives of others.

***Influence begins by accepting the way God made you.***

# CHAPTER 3

# The Conversations of Everyday Influence

conversation

con·ver·sa·tion

kŏn'vər-sā'shən

NOUN

The exchange of thoughts and feelings by means of speech.

\*     \*     \*

Fourth grade (1961-62) flowed into fifth grade (1962-63) and with it its resulting challenges. Physically, I was best described by the term 'husky.' It was no secret. I actually have in my possession a report card where the teacher wrote the following candid opinion: *"Billy is a large child."*

Academically it was simple to summarize the dilemma:

I went from the smartest kid in the fourth grade to the dumbest kid in the fifth grade.

For kids like me they should have developed a special group: *The Sorta Gifted Program* or *The Kinda Accelerated Program*. I was bright enough to move out of the mainstream program, but not quite sharp enough to keep up with my newfound brilliant classmates. A regular staple of the teacher's comments on the back of my report card would be, "Billy is not working up to his capacity." Right. Easy for you to say.

The premise of the Accelerated Program in this suburban Philadelphia school district was straightforward. "Your children will be working at a faster pace than the mainstream fifth graders, thus the use of the word 'accelerated' in the title," our parents were told in a presentation made by that little fireball of enthusiasm, our teacher, Miss Miller, in early September at 'Back to School Night.'

"The schedule works like this," Miss Miller explained. "The class will be doing four-thirds work each academic year, so that in three years, your child will be one full grade level ahead. That means in eighth grade, the students will be doing ninth grade work. We have found this program to be quite successful, especially for students who take the College Preparatory program in high school. A full year for Advanced Placement classes will help them greatly in getting into the college of their choice."

That last point made my parents smile. Would little Billy be the first generation on either side of the family to actually go to college? Like so many Baby Boomer parents, this was something they could have only daydreamed about in their generation, but it seemed quite plausible for their children—assuming their children worked up to their capacity.

Each weekday morning I would wake up, dress, down a bowl of cereal, and walk to William W. H. Davis Elementary, my educational home for the fourth grade with Mrs. Forde and Mr. Cassell. But, I would stand out in front of Davis Elementary, in order to catch the big yellow school bus shuttling me to neighboring Warminster, Pennsylvania, home of Centennial School, location of the Centennial School District's Accelerated Program. This would be my only year at that school, the only exception to schools named after people. I'd be back at William Davis for sixth grade, followed by junior high at Eugene Klinger and high school at William Tennent.

Centennial's Accelerated Program also brought me my first experience with 'changing classes.' I would begin the day with Miss

Miller in her classroom all morning. Lunch was in the cafeteria, recess on the playground. But, the afternoons found our class leaving Miss Miller's room, walking just a few yards down the hall to the next classroom, where Mrs. Berryman was waiting for us. I guess there were so many kinda bright kids in suburban Philadelphia that they needed to offer two full classes to accommodate all of us. Miss Miller would teach subjects like Math and Science, while Mrs. Berryman taught English and Social Studies.

I didn't care much for Mrs. Berryman. She was older and stricter than any other teacher I had up to that point. The word 'stern' comes immediately to mind to best describe her demeanor. Sternness was demonstrated in a number of ways, most notably by her total unwillingness to laugh at my jokes, which put her at a definite disadvantage in my book.

On the other hand, I liked Miss Miller. Actually I liked her a lot. I'll admit it; I was hit hard by a 'schoolboy crush.' This created its own set of problems as I began to misbehave in order to get more of my teacher's attention in the classroom. To this day, I'm not sure if she had this figured out or not, but it seemed like she didn't because as the ultimate 'punishment' for misbehaving, she required me to move my small desk and chair from its spot with the others and put it right next to her large desk up front. Ah, the bliss!

Life with Miss Miller was difficult and I'm not just referring to an eleven-year-old smitten by a seriously older woman. She had been assigned a new challenge—one that proved disastrous. The powers that be had determined that the mainstream classes would continue to learn traditional math, while the Accelerated Programs would, in effect, be the guinea pigs for what was to become known as the 'New Math.' If, by chance, you are unfamiliar with 'New Math' allow me to enlighten you. Many educators agree that it was the greatest educational disaster of the late 1950's—early 1960's. We Americans were in a panic, thanks to the Russian Sputnik, so anything that would give us back our edge over the nasty Soviets was put in play. 'New Math' was to math what the 'New Coke' was to Coca-Cola, a short-term debacle leading to utter failure due to really bad taste.

I am living proof of the 'New Math's' lunacy. Not only did I not get ahead in math, as was promised by entering the Accelerated Program, I got behind. By the eighth grade, I was doing ninth grade work in every other subject, except Math. In the eighth grade, I was doing fifth grade work in Math, along with a classroom full of accelerated mathematic buffoons.

So, my life in a nutshell: I was bused to school, where I was the dumbest kid in the class, facing either the personification of the word 'stern' or the love of my life who had no clue or no interest. I was chubby. I felt like my parents were spending all the available family time on my little sister, so I was aced out of quality home life as well. My social calendar was zero with one notable exception:

Cub Scouts.

Once a week, on Tuesday evenings, Dad would drive me down to the local Episcopal Church, where our neighborhood troop, Pack 26, convened. Mr. Morris, our Cubmaster, a lively middle-aged balding gentleman with a leaning that went more towards music then knots, camping and hiking, would assemble us together so we could sing a song that began with the words:

> *Over hill, over dale,*
> *We will hit the dusty trail.*
> *We're the Cub Scouts of Pack 26!*

His face would explode into an expression of pure joy, as his boys would continue to sing:

> *Wolf or bear, lion, too,*
> *We can do it all for you,*
> *We're the Cub Scouts of Pack 26!*

Clad in our uniforms of navy blue shirts and pants, with the numbers 2 and 6 on red patches with white numbering sewn to our shirt sleeve, for me the penultimate accouterment was the yellow neckerchief, held together by a gold clasp with the Cub Scout crest emblazoned in blue in its center. Wearing my uniform took me to faraway places in my mind. It made me feel like a cross between a nobleman and a gypsy. I remember how relieved I was when my parents learned that Cub Scout uniforms could be purchased in Husky sizes, which meant that I didn't need to be excluded.

We were a relatively new pack in the Cub Scouting world. As 1962 wound down, there was a rumor swirling around that us local Cub Scouts would be having a new event, a big event occurring in the fall that would end up being the highlight of the year. I had visions of a giant campout up in the nearby Pocono Mountains, or perhaps a hike through historic Valley Forge, yet knowing our Cubmaster, I feared it might be a visit to the Academy of Music to hear Eugene Ormandy conduct the Philadelphia Orchestra in a tribute to Vivaldi.

It turns out I was wrong on all counts. "This November," Cubmaster Morris announced with eyes widened and the tiniest projectile of spit that came forth when he said the word 'thisss,' "we will be catching up with some of our other fellow Cub Scout Packs. Pack 26 will be hosting our first ever Pinewood Derby!"

The boys in blue with the yellow kerchiefs went hysterical, enthusiasm erupting in every corner of the church basement. We didn't need windows because the light of car racing shone brightly in the room.

But of course, it was all a grand and glorious mix-up. We unknowingly were confusing the Pinewood Derby with the Soap Box Derby. Our brains were imagining sitting behind the steering wheel of a finely tuned machine built from a former soapbox, racing at super speeds down a hill to heights of victorious adulation. Instead, we were all handed a block of golden blonde wood the size of four Churchill cigars tied together, along with a plastic bag containing four small black wheels, four gray nails that would serve as axles, and three black decals, one saying *Pinewood Derby* and the other two with the number we would place on each side of our vehicle. I was given lucky number 100.

Needless to say, the difference between Soap Box and Pinewood was, as Mark Twain used to say, like the difference between lightning and lightning bug.

"This is a project designed for you to work on at home with you Dad," Cubmaster Morris explained. "You can shave down your block of wood into any design you'd like. You can also paint your car any color you care to, as well. Just be sure to include your decals, especially your number."

This was starting to sound a little better. Sensing the growing interest, Cubmaster Morris pressed on. "On the first Tuesday night of November we will have a special track set up here at the church for you to race on. The track will start about this high," he said while holding his right hand up to the top of his chest, "And then it will make its way down to floor level. You will all have an opportunity to race your car, but once you've been beaten you will be eliminated."

Pausing for added climactic effect, he added, "We will present trophies to those who finish first, second and third."

I had never won a trophy before.

The year before I had won an autographed baseball in a raffle sponsored by my little league team, but instead of the autographs being from anyone famous, it was just signed by all us amazing ten year olds.

When Dad picked me up that night, I was overflowing with excited information about how we were going to make this little wooden car together and that I wanted to paint it red and that my number was 100 and that there would be trophies for the top three winners.

"That's good, Pal," my Dad said in a verbal flurry from the man of few words.

As a light snow began to fall in the Northeast, I knew we were getting closer to November and yet there was nothing done on my racer. The block of wood was still untouched, sitting benignly next to the bag of wheels and decals on the front right corner of my bedroom dresser. I would try to engage Dad in conversation about the need to get this car race-ready, only to be met by my mother's familiar refrain, "Billy, your Dad is tired from working hard all day. Now go upstairs and do your homework—I want to see a better report card from you this next period." I was never completely sure why Dad didn't answer for himself, but even through his interpreter, the message was clear—no work on the racecar right now. And Mom, once again, registered her disappointment in me.

Tuesday, November 6th, was fast approaching and I was beginning to panic. Dad was still not talking and Mom was still translating the silence towards me as business and fatigue related. I was too young to interpret all the psychology that lay underneath that silence. I just knew I wanted my racer transformed.

Fraternizing with my fellow Cub Scouts only made my stomach twist even tighter. "My Dad and I finished my car three weeks ago," one of my friends reported with great pride. "It's gold and it's number 75," he continued. "Dad says we're bringing home the gold with the gold. Get it?" I nodded in concern and jealousy. We've got to get our car done.

Saturday, November 3rd brought a rainy day that turned out to be a perfect day to stay inside and work on a Pinewood Derby racer. "Let's do it," Dad said softly as we made our way downstairs to the basement, home of his collection of tools. I watched him place the block of wood into a vice at the end of his workbench. Using a plane, and then a file, he rounded the edges of the wooden hunk, followed by the soft application of sandpaper.

"It still looks kinda chunky," I opined. "Let's shave it down a little more."

Dad looked up from his sanding and shook his head. My countenance dropped as I imagined all the really cool racecars I would be facing in just a few short days. I remember thinking, "Well, I'm a husky, so I guess my race car will be a husky as well."

Dad placed one of his strong hands on my shoulder and simply said, "*Trust me on this one.*"

My attention was quickly averted as we opened up a can of bright red paint, and we gave the whole car a first coat that appeared to be good enough. While I was admiring our work, Dad had opened up a can of white paint and with the smallest brush we owned, he painted a white swirl down both sides of the racer, as well as on the top. He finished off his artistic flair by painting a small white circle, the diameter of the eraser on the top of a pencil, where the steering wheel would be located on our car. He tousled my hair, gave me a wink and found his way back upstairs to fulfill a list of To-Do's my mother had constructed for the rest of his Saturday.

The next evening, when the paint was fully dry, we applied our decals and the husky red racer was ready for action. I sighed a sigh of relief. We completed the task with 48 hours to spare.

Tuesday night was the most memorable night of my Cub Scout career. It started out in a very bad way, as I strode through the door of the church basement and discovered that what I had daydreamed had become a reality. Just about every car I saw in the hands of my fellow Cub Scouts was sleek and aerodynamically designed. At least that's the way I viewed it.

Quite a few of the racers had been whittled down to a sharp point in the front of the car, which gave it a rocket ship kind of look and feel. The majority of the cars had been painted silver or gold, with a few of us marching to a different drummer by going with the primary colors, now reading quite dull by comparison.

What happened next came at the speed of a gunshot, but nobody in the room could have known what occurred, because it was all happening in my head. Upon seeing all the other racecars, I immediately became embarrassed at my own. It was big, fat and chunky, just like I viewed myself at that time of my life.

Embarrassment led to anger. I was livid at my Dad. "If he had more time to help me with this project, we could have a race car that looks as cool as some of these other ones," I fumed to myself in silence.

I wanted to run away, but it was too late. Cubmaster Morris had already begun assigning us all heats in which our cars would race. Plus, by this time Dad had parked his car and was in the church basement, standing over on the side with all the other fathers. Most of the boys were pleased that their father had been invited to this race. In contrast, I wasn't feeling so warm and fuzzy at that point in the evening.

But as the races began, a fairly obvious phenomenon was exposed. The heavier the car, the faster it went downhill to the finish line. Apparently the Dads who were the Wonderful Whittlers and the Fabulous Filers and the Perfect Planers had disregarded the whole gravity of the situation (pun intended).

Big Red Number 100 was one of the heaviest cars on the track that night. As a matter of fact, only one car could beat it and that was the car that wasn't whittled at all. This square block of wood, obviously thrown together at the last minute was the champion of the evening.

But it didn't really matter to me. Coming in second place still scored me a trophy. They used to call it a Loving Cup. It was gold, about three inches high, standing on a three-inch tall square block of walnut. That six inches of trophy was the crowning achievement of my life for years to come, as I would gaze at it in its place of prominence in my bedroom. A few weeks after the Derby, the engraved gold plate arrived that slid into the front slot of the walnut.

*2nd PRIZE*
*WM. BUTTERWORTH*
*PINEWOOD DERBY*
*1962*
*PACK 26*

Once again my Dad, he of so few words, had put the whole event into perspective when he said to me that Saturday afternoon, "*Trust me on this one.*" Even a man of few words could produce mighty influence with his rare verbal insights.

*       *       *

The Bible is full of verses encouraging us to talk with one another.

*"Hear, O Israel! The Lord is our God, the Lord is one! You shall love the Lord your God with all your heart and with all your soul and with all your might. These words, which I am commanding you today, shall be on your heart. You shall **teach** them diligently to your sons and shall talk of them when you sit in your house and when you walk by the way and when you lie down and when you rise up. You shall bind them as a sign on your hand and they shall be as frontals on your forehead. You shall write them on the doorposts of your house and on your gates.*
—Deuteronomy 6: 4-9 NASB (emphasis added)

Right in the middle of that passage is the word 'teach' which is a more formal way of extolling the value of conversation. The sharing of words back and forth is what separates us from the animals, so why wouldn't we invest in words that create lasting impact?

What is passed along in those conversations is often pure verbal gold. King Solomon knew that to be true. He wrote centuries ago:

*Give instruction to a wise man and he will be still wiser,*
*Teach a righteous man and he will increase his learning.*
—Proverbs 9: 9 NASB

*The teaching of the wise is a fountain of life, To turn aside from the snares of death.*
—Proverbs 13: 14 NASB

*Bright eyes gladden the heart; Good news puts fat on the bones.*
–Proverbs 15: 30 NASB

*The heart of the wise instructs his mouth And adds persuasiveness to his lips. Pleasant words are a honeycomb, Sweet to the soul and healing to the bones.*
—Proverbs 16: 23, 24 NASB

*He kisses the lips Who gives a right answer.*
—Proverbs 24: 26 NASB

I didn't fully realize it at the time, but I was longing to hear more from my father than just the occasional word or phrase. I probably would have kissed his lips if he had given an answer—any answer.

A few years ago I began seeing a therapist about some issues with which I was wrestling in my life. As it goes with most therapists, we made our way back to my parents in pretty short order. I had stuffed down so many emotions about my Mom and Dad for years, but I knew I was ready to uncover the true feelings I held close.

"Describe your feelings towards your mother and father," the therapist began.

"Well," I replied, "this is overstated, I know, but my dad was like my angel and my mom was like my devil."

"Hmmm," came the therapeutically profound response, followed by earnest, even aggressive note taking.

"I could never do anything good enough to please my mother," I explained to the therapist, just knowing for sure that he would have a heyday with that pronouncement.

So we talked a lot about Mom. He led me into telling him about her parents and how she was brought up by a man who was as emotionally big and powerful as he was large and strong in his physique. "Do you think he was a man your mother found difficult to please?" the therapist asked.

"I think he probably was an intimidating guy, whose demands his daughter felt like she could never live up to," I answered, as the dawn of understanding made its way above my mental and emotional horizon. "He probably belittled her."

Thinking I had gained the insight I was meant to gain, I was surprised when the therapist pressed on. "What did you Mom's Mom do when your Mom's Dad would belittle your mother?"

"Nothing," I answered quickly. "She would just stand by and let my grandfather dish it out."

"That wasn't a very kind way for your grandmother to behave towards your mother, was it?"

"No, it wasn't," I replied, not yet fully allowing the weight of that concept to settle in.

"So I have another question for you," the therapist pressed on.

"Okay," I said.

"When your mother would say things that would make you feel like you could never measure up, what did your Dad do?"

I sat silently as my eyes grew moist and talking became a challenge. "Nothing," I whispered. "He just stood there, watching it happen."

We sat without talking for several minutes, the only sound being my labored breathing.

"That's not so good, is it?" I eeked out in barely a whisper.

"Let's look at your dad's upbringing," he replied and before too long we could also discover why he behaved the way he behaved.

"I just wish he would have talked to me more," I confessed. "There's so much about him I'll never know, because he never spoke up."

The therapist nodded compassionately.

"I learned more about my dad at his funeral than I did the whole time I knew him. He was such a mystery."

"I think we all wish we had more conversations with the people we value," the therapist agreed. "If only people knew how influential their words could be in the lives of others."

It's the truth.

Conversations are conduits for everyday influence.

Just like Dad would say:

*Trust me on this one.*

**Influence occurs when I take time to talk.**

# CHAPTER 4

# The Choir of Everyday Influence

choir

choir

kwahy*uh* r

NOUN

An organized group of singers.

\*     \*     \*

The move from Ambler to Southampton instigated all manner of changes in the life of our little family. We went from a one-story house to a two story Colonial. We went from a one car Ford Fairlane family to a two car Ford Galaxy and Ford Falcon family. We went from a Presbyterian Church to a Baptist Church. And it was that last change that would have the most lasting influence in my life.

Both my parents had grown up attending church, my father attending a Lutheran congregation and my mother attending a Baptist flock. When they first married they discovered the First Presbyterian Church of Ambler and that became their church of choice for almost ten years. Well do I remember singing *The Crusader's Hymn* each

Sunday, as well as receiving the small lapel pins given out each year for perfect attendance. Once the first pin was received, a round gold pin with a painted cross in its center surrounded by the words 'Presbyterian SS,' tiny thin golden bars were given out in subsequent years, with the word 'Second Year,' 'Third Year,' and so on as they gave testimony to a life of Sunday mornings in devotion to our God. I remember thinking as a young child that entrance to Heaven would be gained by perfect attendance in Sunday School, so when I died, I would ask to be buried wearing my blue blazer with the all-important lapel pin and its corresponding golden bars worn on it. When St. Peter would ask why I should be allowed in God's Heaven, I would point to my pins, by that time in my life, hanging down below my belly button and reply, "Look, I'm a company man, you've got to let me in!" Duly impressed, St. Peter would willingly agree as he opened the Pearly Gates for me.

Perhaps the grandest occasion for a Presbyterian child in Ambler was the day he was given his own copy of the Bible. This was no small accomplishment and as a result, this was no ordinary Bible one was presented. The typical Bible of the day was bound in black leather with gold leaf on the pages. But when a child at First Presbyterian Church of Ambler was honored with his own copy of the Bible, it was a Bible in white leather (fake leather, let's be honest) with a gold zipper surrounding the gold leaf pages, allowing the Bible to be bound tight so all one's bookmarks, note cards and pictures of Jesus could remain in the Bible without falling out. The unique appearance of this particular Bible was capstoned by the small gold cross that was at the end of the zipper. Stamped in gold across the front cover were the words *Holy Bible*, which I had automatically assumed, since there had never been another book in my life that was in faux white leather with a gold zipper and matching gold cross at the zipper's end. Of course it was holy.

The move to Southampton in my fourth grade year brought us to a fork in the religious road. I'm not sure why the First Presbyterian Church of Southampton didn't become our church of choice—oh yeah, now I remember—there was no First Presbyterian Church of Southampton.

The denomination was well represented in the neighboring towns of Northampton and Ivyland, but let's face it, convenience trumped theology every time, so we converted from quiet Presbyterians to quiet Baptists. I emphasize the word 'quiet' because in my family demonstrative acts of religion were frowned upon. *Never discuss politics or religion* was just as crucial to survival of the human race as was *children should be seen and not heard.*

The Baptist Church was a three-minute drive from our house. It was a slam-dunk in the convenience category so we joined up right away. Before I knew it, I was introduced to a way to do church I had not previously experienced. What a Presbyterian can cover in one Sunday service, the Baptists needed all week to handle. Gone were the days of little Billy attending Sunday School while Mommy and Daddy were in Big Church. Now, we all attended age appropriate Sunday School services at 9:30 Sunday morning, followed by us all attending Big Church together at 11:00. But wait, there's more! Sunday evening began at 6 P.M. with 'Youth Group,' a special program, again divided up to be age appropriate. At 7:15 it was Sunday Evening Church, always beginning with the congregation singing the John W. Peterson chorus,

> *Coming Again, Coming Again,*
> *May be morning, may be noon, may be evening and may be soon,*
> *Coming Again, Coming Again*
> *Oh what a wonderful day that will be,*
> *Jesus is coming again!*

In the summers, after Sunday Evening Church, the youth would be loaded into a old yellow bus and transported to a neutral site where many churches would converge for a Sunday Evening Hymn-sing.

One might think a full day of Church would be sufficient, even for a Baptist, but we were just getting started. Monday night was our night of rest because the remainder of the week was jammed. Tuesday night was centered on Boy's Brigade, our Church's version of Boy

Scouts. Wednesday night the whole family gathered back together for Prayer Meeting. Thursday night was Church Choir practice, which my mother, queen of the sopranos, took as seriously as a heart attack. There was usually a Friday night function for the youth, perhaps bowling or miniature golf or if it was winter maybe some ice-skating. Saturday was Children's Choir practice, until I was old enough for Youth Choir practice, again held on Saturday mornings. Then we were back to Sunday, the day of Sabbath rest.

Since my mother was such a committed soprano, I had no choice but to join the choir. Unlike the fourth grade Chorus, under the direction of Mr. Cassell, this Children's Choir in the church had a particular wrinkle that I found somewhat distasteful.

I was the only boy.

That's right, it was an all-girl ensemble until Little Billy showed up. Being young enough to be a boy soprano, the musical side of the equation was not the issue as much as the social side. Elementary school boys are not usually known for their love of the female gender and I was no exception. Children's choir was cruel and inhuman punishment to me, but my mother would have it no other way. "Stop your complaining," she'd snap at me. "There are children in China who have nothing to eat, so go up and do your homework so you can make better grades!" Her logic always escaped me. And of course, Dad was still silent, so what else could she do? Mom continued her dutiful role as the only Parental Voice.

Sensing my reluctance to be a part of an all-girls group, our Children's Choir director, Mrs. Heath, took pity on me. It was a glorious day when she took me aside and said to me, "Billy, we really are so glad you are in our choir. I know you are a really strong soprano, but I'm wondering if you would consider singing with the altos? We need a powerful voice like yours to carry that all-important harmony part."

Of course, alto is still a girl's part, but the way she phrased the question made me feel like a basso profundo. "Yes, Mrs. Heath, I'll join the altos," I said, with a newfound degree of confidence. These girls needed me and I've got to carry my load.

Upon entering junior high it was time to be promoted from Children's Choir to Youth Choir. Just like moving from king of the elementary school to pawn of the junior high, I was no longer the king of the altos. I was a tenor, the youngest tenor, in a choir made up of teenagers, the musical world's most dangerous grouping. Singing was still a girl's territory, best seen by the fact that the girls were divided into soprano and alto, whereas the guys were all called baritones. Basses and tenors would be acknowledged if and when one chose to enter the adult choir, upon high school graduation.

The Youth Choir director was Mr. Doyle, a smallish man with jet black hair, graying temples, the biggest black glasses with the thickest magnifying lens I had ever seen, all resting on the tiniest little nose. None of us could figure out why those glasses didn't fall down around his chin, since there was no visible nose to speak of, when those supersized specs rested on it. Like Mr. Cassell, he loved music and he passed along that love to all of us through his genuine enthusiasm for each and every song we sang.

Naturally, the highlights of the Church Choir year were Christmas and Easter. Like so many churches of that time, our Choir would perform a Cantata for each season, a collection of ten or twelve songs, woven together by narration walking us through the story of Christ's birth or His death, burial and resurrection. The King of the Church Cantata was a man named John W. Peterson. Each year, he would premiere a new cantata for each holiday, and the average Church choir director would buy it right up, excitedly sharing it with his choir.

The Christmas and Easter Cantatas were special for another reason—Mr. Doyle would allow the Youth Choir to join the Adult Choir, giving the combined choirs a broader, more majestic sound.

Growing up singing the music of John Peterson was an enriching experience for me. Years later, in 1976, I was able to meet him in person and you would have thought I was shaking hands with Johann Sebastian Bach, Martin Luther, or Paul McCartney, I was so nervous.

My parents took to the social aspect of the Baptist Church like ducks to water. It was the Country Club of choice for blue-collar families. A place to spend every available hour of the week, without initiation fees (but of course there would be the offering at every meeting) and no snobbery about who can and who cannot become a member.

For me, church was something my parents seemed to enjoy, so I did my best to find friends and give it my best shot. Billy Holmes, my best friend in Ambler, became replaced by Billy Reiss, my new best friend in Southampton. He would soon change churches, but fortunately Bobby Harron was there to pick up the slack.

Regarding my spiritual condition at the time, the best way to describe it was that I just went through the motions at church. I knew when to stand in the service. I knew when to sit. Besides the proper postures, I also knew the hymns and the choruses. But it was superficial to me, at best. God was real. Jesus was real. There just wasn't much of a connection for me as my life transitioned from child to adolescent.

All of that was to change the summer between my junior and senior year in high school. The Church hired a new Youth Pastor and this one was different from the previous line up of usual suspects that rode the merry-go-round on our Church staff. His name was Ron Von Behren, Ron Von, for short. The big deal to all of us was that he came from Florida. Most of the previous Youth Pastors were local folks, brought in from the nearby Bible College, but we did have a terrible reputation as the youth group that could chew them up and spit them out faster than any other young congregation in the Northeast.

We were to discover that Ron Von was different. Along with his wife Debbie and their daughter Kerry, Ron Von possessed a zeal that was off the chart in his desire to see his teenage flock embrace the Lord with a greater depth and knowledge than we had ever experienced.

It was tough sledding to begin with for the Von Behrens. We felt that it was our Christian duty to make their life miserable, whether it was letting the air out of their tires, or soaping their windows, or gaining entrance into their humble apartment and short-sheeting their bed. But Ron Von became what I describe as 'the pit bull of love.' He was determined to get through to us and he had a secret plan that was certain to get our youth group on board.

"How would you guys like to go to a Christian Conference in south Florida for two weeks this summer?" was the question he posed. This offer caught our attention. Most of us didn't really hear the words 'Christian Conference.' All we heard was 'two weeks in south Florida.' I was working a summer job at the local grocery store, stocking shelves, so I didn't have a whole lot going on socially. A few of my friends from outside the church had offered me a spot in their car heading up to some big music festival in a field in a town called Woodstock, New York. But South Florida beaches sounded more appealing than northern New York farm fields, so the choice was an easy one for me. By the time we were ready to make the long journey, Ron Von had thirty of us signed up for the full two weeks of what became known as Bible Camp.

We arrived in Boca Raton, Florida at a very suspicious destination. *Welcome To Bibletown* the sign read and thirty teenagers proceeded to fall into panic mode. Once calm had been restored, we stood in line at the only pay phone we could find. One by one we each called our parents—collect, of course—and demanded money for a flight home. We had been deceived, we said. Our visions of surf, sand, and fun were going to be stifled by a litany of daily Bible meetings being held in the mornings and the evenings. Some of our group became even more dramatic, suggesting we were going to be brainwashed into some foreign cult. We must be released from this horrible imprisonment, they pled with their parents.

Not one parent bought it. All thirty of us were severely lectured by our parents on the importance of being good boys and girls, paying attention to what the teachers taught us. Or else.

Amazingly, we did as we were told.

Paying attention changed the direction of our lives.

For the first time in my life, I came to understand the message of the Gospel. It's ironic that I sat in church all those Sundays (Tuesdays,

Wednesdays, Thursdays, Fridays, and Saturdays, too) and I'm certain if I had just paid attention one time, I would have heard the same message. But it was during that two week stay in Boca Raton, Florida that I understood that Jesus, the Savior of the world, wanted to be Jesus, my personal Savior. The teachers hit that message hard from the beginning of the week. By Wednesday, I had the Gospel message firmly planted deep within my heart.

I had heard some of the other kids at this conference speaking in hushed tones about how special Wednesday night was going to be because it was 'Dedication Night.' I was sufficiently confused as to what that meant and why it was to be so significant. Perhaps parents were bringing in their babies to be dedicated, I mused or maybe the conference center was buying a new pipe organ and wanted it dedicated. Wednesday evening arrived and I was still quite unclear on the issue as I headed to the auditorium.

"Tonight," our teacher began, "I want to give you an opportunity to stand from your seat, come forward to the front of the auditorium and publicly dedicate your life to serve Jesus Christ with all your heart." He made a strong point that we serve Christ, not to earn our salvation, but because He has saved us. "We serve Him out of love" he explained. At the end of his talk, he asked us to bow our heads and close our eyes. "Who will stand and come forward this evening?"

Unlike I had ever felt before, God was clearly tugging on my heart. If I had any reservation about standing and coming forward, it disappeared as *dozens* of kids my age immediately stood to their feet and made their way down front. I would not be an oddball by making my stand for the Lord. I did it wholeheartedly.

The rest of the week included teaching on how to pray, how to tell others about Jesus and how to study the Bible (I took the opportunity to purchase a new Bible in basic black at their bookstore. Being a teenage boy with a white Bible with gold zipper just seemed to be sending the wrong message).

Friday night was a repeat of Wednesday night, another message on dedicating your life to the Lord for those who had held back two nights before. Staying in Florida for two weeks meant that our merry band of 30 Pennsylvanians experienced the entire week of camp twice, since each week had been set up identically. But Ron Von knew what he was doing. He used the second week as a week to strategize with the 30 of us about going back home and reaching our high school with the Gospel. We talked of forming a Thursday night meeting that would include singing with guitars, skits, and then Ron Von would give a brief message with the plan of salvation. It was an amazing time for me. It felt like we were the original twelve in the Upper Room that week, as we honestly believed we could win the whole world.

Driving back in the van from Florida, Ron Von asked me to sit up front by him for part of the journey. "We're going to need leaders for our Thursday night meeting and I'm hoping you will be one of them," Ron Von explained as we passed yet one more sign for *South of the Border* on Interstate 95 in scenic South Carolina.

"What do you need me to do?" I asked, wanting to be completely on board, but still feeling some hesitancy in my soul.

"We need someone to lead the songs each week," he pressed on. "You are great on the guitar, you know the music, you have real leadership abilities, you're the man," Ron Von gushed.

As complimented as I was, I still wasn't sure that this was the right job for me. "I need to think about it," I told him, my reluctance bleeding through.

Unaffected by my response he quickly added, "Sure, Bill. That's okay. Anyway, if you don't do it, I can do it."

My entire body tensed up with his last statement. Ron Von was so good at so many things, but he was also equally bad at many things as well. On the top of his bad list was 'singing.' In musical terminology, Ron Von was a monotone; best defined by the quaint little phrase 'he can't carry a tune in a bucket.'

The ride home from Florida was a long one. Haunted by the thought of Ron Von and his deep, flat, loud voice singing *Kum Ba Yah* with each note sounding the same, I felt I had no choice but to agree to lead the singing on Thursday nights. Ron Von was thrilled. "I'll sit on a stool right next to you and I'll play my guitar," he volunteered.

"Just promise me you won't sing," I countered.

"You've got a deal," he beamed, holding out his hand for the obligatory handshake.

Little did I realize at the time that Ron Von was establishing a pattern with our group. We all genuinely loved him, but we were also painfully aware of his shortcomings. So when he asked for volunteers to act in the skits—and nobody would volunteer—he would say that he would do it himself. Ron Von had the chemistry to be in skits that one would associate with such great skit actors as Genghis Khan or Prince Charles. Accordingly, we all lined up for skit duty week after week.

The longer we worked with Ron Von the more we became aware of what we ended up calling his leadership style: *Ron Von's gift is that he has no gift.* He seemed extraordinarily successful in moving his followers up into leadership positions, because most of us knew if we didn't take the position, he would, and it would be awkward at best, a disaster at worst.

That committed band of 30 began our Thursday night meetings and by the third week we had 380 of our fellow high schoolers in attendance. I have to admit, I have never been in something so amazing in my life. It was Ron Von's faithful influence during my senior year that also caused me to change my college plans from majoring in Business at Penn State to a degree in Biblical Education from Florida Bible College.

*       *       *

I have much to be thankful for in the history I have with the local church. More deeply than most, I understand the admonition from the writer of the New Testament book of Hebrews:

*Not forsaking our own assembling together, as is the habit of some, but encouraging one another; and all the more as you see the day drawing near.*
—Hebrews 10: 25 NASB

When people get together, people influence, whether they mean to or not. What Mrs. Heath, Mr. Doyle and Ron Von did for me equates to powerful impact, yet I wonder if they even know what they accomplished in my life. That trio, woven together through the tapestry of music, marked me for years and years to come.

A lot happened in my life thanks to that Choir of teachers—Mrs. Heath, Mr. Doyle and Ron Von. Music was its common thread but quiet influence outshone musical knowledge.

**Influence occurs in the presence of others.**

# CHAPTER 5

# The College
# of Everyday
# Influence

college

col-lege

kol-ij

kalij

NOUN

An educational institution providing higher education.

*　　*　　*

Iigh school graduation in 1970 suburban Philadelphia included just the earliest beginnings of hippies, drugs and rock and roll. What had swept the country for several years was somewhat slow in making its way to Southampton. However, all of the girls were wearing mini-skirts, while most of the guys refrained from long hair, choosing instead the long, wide sideburns referred to as 'mutton chops' a century before. The traditional graduation caps and gowns covered most of our non-conformity and protestations. In a fitting tribute to the word 'bland' our high school colors were black and white. The closest we got to anything outlandishly contemporary was standing at the end of the ceremony, holding hands and singing Carole King's *You've Got a Friend.*

There was a genuine excitement inside of me about going to college in south Florida. My white 1966 Ford Fairlane was packed to the gills as I left home for the 24-hour road trip down Interstate 95 that blistering hot summer. The car was so full of stuff, nothing could be seen out of any windows but the front windshield and the window to my left, leaving all the side and rear viewing to emanate from a single slice of the left side mirror. It was a good thing the car was packed full, however, because upon making my first trip back to Pennsylvania that Christmas, I was to discover that all the rest of my belongings had mysteriously disappeared, as a result of my parents turning my bedroom into a 'sewing room.' This development grieved me on several levels, not the least of which was that neither of my parents sewed.

I was not alone heading off to Miami from Southampton. Ron Von had influenced so many of us in our higher education decisions that we arrived at Bible College that year like already established Fraternities and Sororities. It certainly made the transition easier, going off to college with a bunch of your friends accompanying you. Not only was I part of a group of friends, I had become somewhat of a leader among them. Ron Von had poured hours of his life into mine so that during my senior year of high school I was more than his song leader; I was his right hand man.

Thus, one would think I entered college brimming with self-confidence. An already established leader with a merry band of friends accompanying me, it certainly gave the appearance that this was one cool guy. Looks can be so deceiving. Even though at that age I was tall and thin, inside it was still the little fat kid, filled with struggle and that struggle made the move with me to Florida.

For example, consider my inability to figure out girls. I really didn't date in high school and it wasn't because I had no interest. I was smitten like every other boy with the girls who would compete for Homecoming Queen, as well as the entire Cheerleading Squad, yet I never felt secure enough in myself to ask any of them out. I was convinced that none of them would have interest in the little fat kid.

I had a little bit of success as an alternate date, however. Like a seat-filler at an awards show, I substituted for the celebrity when they needed to use the rest room. I dated Pam when she broke up with Gary, but it took only one date for them to realize they were made for each other, so one date was all I'd get. The same thing goes for Denise going out with me when she broke up with Nelson or Dee and I on a date because she broke up with Ted. Clearly, dating was not my strongest suit.

Having come out of a church youth group that used me in a musical leadership position, I screwed up enough courage to audition for *The Internationals,* the musical group that was considered the 'official group' at the college. To my amazement, I passed the audition, but it didn't take me long to figure out why. The director wasn't so much impressed with my musical leadership as he was quite fixated on the fact that back in Pennsylvania I had participated in so many *skits.* My acceptance into this group had virtually nothing to do with musical expertise, but everything to do with my ability to write and perform a skit towards the end of each concert that would spotlight the fact that we would be selling record albums in the back of the room after the concert. Branded in my mind is how all of us singers would come close to our microphones, each of us leaning into the mike atop a thin silver metal stand, and yet I can still see the director, while waving his arms to direct, using his right hand to signal that I was too close to my mike, so step back, young man, step back.

Class elections came up early in my freshman year and with my merry band of Pennsylvanians, I thought I had a shot at winning Class President. In what would end up being a pattern for me throughout college, I came in second place, thus I was easily elected Freshman Class Vice President, which was Student Government lingo for close, but no cigar.

The musical group I sold records for at the college was an officially sponsored entity of the college, but there were a wide variety of smaller groups developed by students and faculty alike. These smaller groups usually consisted of some guitars and bass players backing up five or six singers. Being the 70's at a Bible College, these groups had names like *The Spokesmen, Bold Generation, The Joyful Noise,* and *The Sound of Truth.* There was a clear pecking order to these groups and it was *The Spokesmen* that claimed the top of the pile. An all-male group, these six guys had two guitars, a bass, plus a keyboard player and a drummer. They were the group to be a part of. I made no secret of the fact that I wanted to be a *Spokesman* more than anything,

But it didn't happen.

In my sophomore year, with no interest from *The Spokesmen* and no interest in going back to skits selling records, I acted on a surprisingly courageous impulse and formed my own group. Three guys, three girls, one guitar and a bass player we came up with the name *Free Joy*, which at the time we felt was no cooler or no stupider than any of the other group names on campus. The six of us worked hard and we became a popular group, arguably the second best group on campus. But we couldn't overtake *The Spokesmen.*

By the end of my junior year I was, from all outward appearances, in a very good place. I was President of my class, our group had cut an album in Nashville, I was dating a pretty girl, I seemed to be respected and appreciated around the campus by students and faculty alike. But it was still tumultuous inside. I wasn't happy with myself and it impacted the way I processed everything.

At the end of my junior year it was time for Student Government elections for the following year. The big prize was Student Body President, a position that not only brought with it prestige and honor, but a full scholarship as well. Having spent the last three years working at least one, if not two jobs simultaneously in order to pay for college, Student Body President was the ideal position for me. And history was on my side. The precedent favored the Junior Class President winning the position in almost every instance. With all these favorable factoids in my pocket, I threw my hat in the ring and looked forward to Election Day.

There was one surprise as I glanced over the list of nominees. In a move that was completely out of left field, there was a name of a guy who I believed to be a sophomore who decided to run against me for the coveted top position. This made no sense to me—he should run for Junior Class President and wait his turn to be Student Body President his senior year.

"He's a transfer student, so he'll be a senior next year," fellow classmates clarified for me. "Don't worry, he won't win." I took their advice by not giving it too much thought.

I had all of the upcoming summer as well as the following academic year to give it a lot more thought as the unthinkable occurred. He beat me. Victorious in his run for Student Body President, I was left with the Student Government Consolation Prize—Senior Class President.

The Bible College was in the midst of a growth spurt during these years and as a result, they were doing a lot of hiring, bringing in new faculty members in record numbers. Unlike most academic institutions, this school prided itself in not bringing in outsiders, but training up its own 'homegrown' talent and using them so they won't get 'negatively impacted' somewhere else. Unquestionably it was a very unhealthy way to create a faculty, I now understand, but as a senior at the college, I set my sights on a new ultimate prize—a position on the faculty.

I wanted to be the only senior offered a job. That way I would show all my peers that I was far and away the best member of the entire student body—so take that all the rest of you!

My wish came true. Sort of.

I did get ushered into the President's office and offered a fulltime position on the faculty, beginning immediately after graduation. I would teach Summer School, help in the Summer Camps the College sponsored and then gear up for the big Fall and Spring Semesters. Allowing the President to gush over my record during my four years at the college, I was welling up with pride and that exhilarating feeling of accomplishment. Achieving my goal was a big deal, so it should not have hurt me so much when the interview ended with the President saying to me, "We're glad you're joining the team, Bill. And you'll be glad to know we are going to extend the same invitation to your good friend Gary. What a one-two punch you guys are going to be!"

I smiled the sickly smile of politeness as my mind raced. "Gary! Why would they want to hire Gary when they've got me?"

On the positive side, summer school was an epiphany as I discovered how much I loved teaching. The classroom energized me, and seeing students, who just a few weeks ago were my classmates, learning and growing brought me a deep satisfaction that I could not deny. Between summer school and fall semester was the summer camp season, three weeks of camp in the model of my experience up in Boca Raton five years earlier. As a new faculty member, I was now eligible to be one of the teachers during those three summer weeks, and I was pleasantly surprised to be chosen for two sessions each week. "We've got you on the schedule for Monday morning and Wednesday morning," the camp director explained. "With your teaching style, you are perfect for early in the week." There was no interpretation necessary. Like I had been chosen for the college music group, I was being placed on the teaching team as a result of my ability to use humor, not necessarily because I brought any real knowledge of the subjects I was to teach. This was not a bad thing, but because I was not yet at a place to understand it I came to despise my strength as 'the funny guy' to the point that a few years later I was doing everything I could to 'not be funny' while speaking. It was so opposite of God's design for me that I was literally throwing up before each class or speaking session, so certain that I couldn't be taken seriously no matter how I tried.

Summer camp was no exception. In my Monday and Wednesday sessions the audience was roaring with laughter as I regaled them of stories from my youth. The greater objective was being achieved—we were gaining acceptance from these kids and they were becoming much more open to the more serious teaching that would come later in the week. It was the exact same pattern that had been so effective in my life five years earlier, yet I was so blinded by my own agendas, I couldn't see the beauty of the plan.

This particular dilemma climaxed at the end of the third week of camp. All of the teaching sessions were recorded and made available for purchase in the Bookstore. The campers were encouraged to buy the cassettes, take them home and replay them in order to further cement the teachings that had occurred during the week. A young girl, probably fifteen years old, approached me during the last day of camp with a question. "I only have enough money for one more tape and I want it to be one of yours," she began, as I did my best not to blush at the complimentary thought. "So could you tell me which tape you think I should buy?"

Knowing the camp strategy, I launched into the expected answer. "Well, the later we get in the week, the more teaching we give. So, for my two sessions, the Wednesday tape is going to be much more informative than the Monday tape," I explained.

"Oh, you don't understand," she replied, her eyes widening and freckles freckling. "If I want teaching tapes I always buy tapes from the last two days. I want to know which of your tapes do you think is the *funniest*?"

Feeling like I was going to throw up caused me to give her the briefest of answers. "Monday is funnier than Wednesday. Go get a Monday tape."

She ran off to the Bookstore, all smiles, while I ran off to the Men's Room, all contorted.

"She wanted your tapes," I said to myself in the rest room, splashing cold water on my face, in an effort to be consoling. "But only because they were funny," I added, wadding up the wet paper towel and tossing it into the can with the force of a cannon.

*     *     *

The dictionary defines 'college' as 'an educational institution providing higher education.' Most of us learn a lot more during our years in college beyond the classroom. For me, it was a time of paradox. Seemingly I was a happy-go-lucky guy, well liked, funny, musical, respected by my peers and my leaders, yet inside my heart was troubled. Uncomfortable in my own skin, I had some major work I had to do on the inside.

A few years after my start as a teacher at the Bible College, God brought two men into my life that ended up influencing me as deeply as any men I had ever been with. Through them, the healing began. One man I first met only through his cassette tapes, but I became instantly attracted to him due to his engaging teaching style. His name was Howard Hendricks, a professor at Dallas Seminary, where he was affectionately known as Prof. I purchased one of his tapes, simply titled *Motivation* and ended up listening to it over and over again. It was so good I ended up playing it every semester for every class I taught. The depth of content was unmistakable, but there was something else that was screaming at me from the cassette recorder: *this guy was hilarious and he was making no apology for his humor!*

As time progressed at the Bible College, there was a regime change and the new President, unlike his predecessor, encouraged further education for its faculty. I immediately applied and was accepted at Dallas Theological Seminary where I majored in Prof. Hendricks. Even though he was shorter and balder than he sounded on tape, I instantaneously fell in love with this guy—who wouldn't? I discovered that Prof grew up in Philadelphia—not the suburbs like me, but in the city, like my Dad. Years later, upon further investigation, I uncovered the fact that my Dad and Prof went to the same high school—Northeast High School for Boys! Dad was a senior when Prof was a freshman, but what are the odds that two men who would influence my life so profoundly at two different times in my life literally grew up in the same inner-city neighborhood and went to the same school together?

The more I studied under Prof, the more comfortable I felt in the way God had gifted me. He could use me, just the way He made me, to be of impact in the lives of others, and that included the gift of humor He placed within me. Laughter was not a curse, it was a blessing.

This lesson was underscored even more deeply through my relationship with another man who came into my life right about the same time. In the spring of 1976, one of the Board members of the College, seeing the malaise that had developed among the students and faculty, suggested we bring in a friend of his who could speak in Chapel for almost an entire week. None of us had ever heard of this guy, other than he was a Pastor from the West Coast, as far from Florida as one could get in the continental United States. We figured the distance might give him a better perspective on how to encourage us.

He arrived on campus around dinnertime on a Monday evening. Guest housing was in the same building as Faculty housing—a twelve-story high-rise condominium. He ended up on the same floor as my wife and me. Around 6 P.M. there was a knock on our door. Opening it, I saw a man in his forties, silver framed glasses, piercing eyes, strong arms partially hidden under a Hawaiian type shirt that would have been viewed as quite outlandish at the Bible College at that time. What really caught my attention was his hair. It appeared to be styled, perfectly parted, and most importantly, the hair on both sides of his head covered the top half of each ear. In our uptight Bible College world, hair over the ears made this gentleman a cross between John Lennon and Jerry Rubin.

"Hi," he began, his face erupting into a warm smile that no one could resist. "I'm here to speak in Chapel tomorrow and I suddenly realized I don't know what time it starts. I was wondering if you might know and if you could tell me?"

"Come in," I invited, feeling embarrassed that he was to speak tomorrow and was not fully brought up to speed. "My name is Bill Butterworth," I said, offering my hand for a manly shake. "I'm on the Faculty here."

"I'm Chuck Swindoll," he replied in a voice that was stronger than most, grabbing my hand and squeezing it tighter than most.

"Have you had dinner?" I quizzed.

"No, I haven't," he admitted. "Just peanuts on the airplane," he laughed. There was something about that laugh. Big, full, warm, contagious.

"Join us," I replied, introducing him to my wife.

"It's only spaghetti," she confessed, "but there's plenty.

Chuck sat down at our dinner table and thus began a relationship that continues to this day. His Chapel messages were spot on, encouraging weary students and teachers to press on, reaching for the prize, not fainting or losing focus, but enduring.

The only thing I recall more than the admonitions was the style in which it was presented. This guy was funny. He told stories that brought us to tears with our laughter. And, like Prof, no apologies. The big difference between his humor and Prof's was after each punch line, whereas Prof would offer silence, allowing the audience laughter to fill the room, Chuck would deliver the laugh line and before anyone else could respond, he himself would break into the most winsome laugh one has ever heard. Clearly, he didn't take himself too seriously.

*Take God seriously but don't take yourself so seriously* has become my response when someone asks me to describe what Chuck Swindoll is really like. We continued our bi-coastal relationship for several years until he and his wife Cynthia offered me a job at their new radio ministry, *Insight for Living*. Accepting without hesitation, the entire Butterworth family moved from Hollywood, Florida to Fullerton, California to commence a new chapter in our lives.

*　　*　　*

Prof and Chuck helped me see myself for the way God made me, not in comparison or contrast to others. The Apostle Paul addressed this issue by writing:

*For we are not bold to class or compare ourselves with some of those who commend themselves; but when they measure themselves by themselves and compare themselves with themselves, they are without understanding.*
—2 Corinthians 10:12 NASB

Comparing oneself with others only leads to frustration and ulcers. Thank the Lord for godly men who came into my life and in doing so, straightened out some pretty crooked thinking.

We all have Profs and Chucks in our lives and even more amazingly we are a Prof or a Chuck in the lives of others. We may see those others every single day of our lives or we may never know who those others are. The important point is that they exist and we need to take our responsibility seriously.

The influence of Prof and Chuck is unmistakable in my life. A struggling young man found his niche, his place, his calling, all based on the way God had wired him. I imagine neither of those two guys would have thought they were doing anything out of the ordinary. They befriended me, and as a result, they built confidence into my life. In many respects, it was a better education than four years in college.

*Influence expands once we make peace with ourselves.*

# CHAPTER 6

# The Components of Everyday Influence

component

com·po·nent

kəm-ˈpō-nənt

NOUN

One of the parts of something (such as a system or mixture): an important piece of something.

*     *     *

Possessing the athletic ability of a doorknob, to think of me in a sport's context is akin to Pavarotti pole dancing or Bill Gates in the UFC octagon. But I've always loved sports and all my life I've lamented the fact that I was not better suited for them.

In junior high and high school, I joined the track team as a shot putter and discus thrower. This decision was influenced, in a heavy way, by the fact that back in seventh grade I was in a heavy way. "If you could get your beef behind that thing, you could send it into orbit," my shot put coach would implore. Most of my fellow putters and throwers were linemen from the football team and this was their way to stay in shape during the off-season. Comparing myself to these linemen became an exercise in contrasts.

Unlike me, they had strength.

All I had was tonnage. It was a sad state, to say the least. Add to this tale of woe that shortly after I joined the track team, I experienced a growth spurt coupled with a major weight loss. Over one brief summer the short, fat, shot putter became tall and thin. And still with no strength.

But I weathered on, lifting weights every day, retrieving shot puts for stronger guys and in fact eventually receiving a varsity letter, which I deserved, not so much for performance but more for perfect attendance.

The summer of 1970 found me driving from my boyhood home outside Philadelphia to my home for the next decade in sunny south Florida. I would make a pit stop in Dallas for grad school during that decade, but for the lion's share of the time, my mailing address was Hollywood, Florida.

I didn't participate in any sports during my years in Bible College. Even at a small private college, there just didn't seem to be a demand for tall, thin and weak on any team's squad. But there was a sport that enjoyed great popularity at the college that I had never played until those college years.

Tennis.

The first time I stepped onto the court, I was immediately impressed with how this game aligned with my skills. Apparently, if you hit the ball at the proper spot on the strings of the classic wooden racket, you didn't need strength. Check. You could play singles, meaning there was no one else on your team who would belittle you if you missed an important shot. Check. The predominant color in tennis was white—white balls, white shoes, white socks, white shorts, white shirts, white wristbands. Add to that the fact that my hair is white and my skin is whiter than that ream of paper in your printer made me the perfect color for the game. Check.

I wasn't very good at the game, but quickly compensated by only playing others who were of equal tennis horror. It's the only game I know where you can constantly miss shots yet people still scream out, "LOVE!"

A few years after I discovered tennis, I was dating a pretty young lady who would eventually become my wife. We were polar opposites—she was a girl, I was a boy. She was attractive, I was tall, thin and weak. She was athletic, I was a good reader.

We began playing tennis every afternoon around 4:30. Typically we'd play for about an hour, whereupon she would become bored with the constant winning on her side of the net, so we'd retire to dinner. I want to say I let her win, but I've said too much already.

Before too long, we discovered that tennis could be played by both of us on the same team. We discovered doubles. I quickly took to this new twist on an old game. With half of the court to cover, as opposed to the full court, one would think I improved. Well, we did improve, but it was more about me deferring most of the action to her, and watching her put our opponents away. My doubles strategy was quite simple—*stay out of the way!*

Fast forward to the end of that decade. By 1979, we had traded the all-white version of tennis for loud, vibrant, multi-colored outfits with no hint of white anywhere to be found. Even the tennis balls themselves had evolved from boring white to hot, fiery, fluorescent yellow. Wooden rackets were the stuff of the one dollar box at garage sales, traded in for aerodynamic metal rackets glimmering in shiny silver. Yes, the accouterment of the game had changed, but my playing ability had remained at a constant 'definite need for improvement.'

So imagine my utter shock when a friend of mine approached me with the following offer: "Bill, we're cooking up a fundraiser to raise money to help some underprivileged high school kids go to summer camp. There are so many teenagers who want to attend our camp, but just don't have the funds. We want to offer scholarships to them. Knowing you are a big believer in what we're doing, I am hoping you would consider joining us in our event."

"What's your event?" I asked innocently.

"We're going to put on a tennis marathon," was his answer.

"Sounds cool," I replied. "Do you need me to make a pledge or something?"

"No," he answered, followed by a long pause. "I need you to be one of the tennis players."

Still not catching on to the format, I responded with, "Sure. Are you signing people up to play for an hour at a time or something like that?"

"Nope. It's just gonna be four of us."

"And you want me to be one of the four?" I asked incredulously.

"Yes," he answered.

"How long is this marathon?" I inquired.

"We're gonna play 24 hours of tennis," he declared, averting his glance as he said it. I guess he hoped if we didn't have eye contact, it wouldn't sound so ludicrous. By the way, you know who this guy is—it's Ron Von—the guy whose gift is that he has no gift. He, too, had made his way to Florida from Pennsylvania.

"Who are the other three that you've conned into this?" I pressed.

"My friend, Jeff will play with me as one team. And I thought I'd pair you with Shaf."

This was the first piece of good news I had heard since Ron Von opened his mouth. Mike Shaffer, affectionately known as Shaf, (rhymes with chafe, not chaff) was a good friend of mine who was the consummate athlete. He grew up in Atlanta, and as a high school graduate, he went to Georgia Tech on a full football scholarship as a receiver. He was strong, quick, agile, enduring and many other qualities athletes possess that I didn't.

"So let's say I was willing to do this," I postulated to Ron Von, "exactly how is it going to happen?"

Ron Von smiled, a knowing smile that said, *I gotcha*. If I was asking for more information, I was as good as on the court. "Here's the date," he said to me, showing me his calendar. "It's a Friday. We will begin at 10 A.M., right after the morning chapel service is over. We'll announce what's going on and we're hoping the whole student body will come out to start us off with a bang and of course, some helpful donations."

"That's smart," I had to admit.

"Then we will play 55 minutes of tennis every hour. We'll take a five minute break five minutes before the top of each hour and then we'll start up again as the clock chimes. We'll be finished at 10 A.M. Saturday morning, hopefully with a lot of money raised for deserving kids to go to camp."

I still don't know why Ron Von picked me. Just like I still don't know why I agreed to do it. But before I fully comprehended the immensity of the task at hand, I had agreed to play 24 consecutive hours of tennis.

Once I was home I told my wife and as the real athlete in the family, she did her best to be encouraging, but to be honest, it's difficult to be an encourager when you just can't stop yourself from laughing.

We were all busy guys back then, so before we knew it, the fateful Friday in the center of the spring arrived and it was time to play tennis. Ron Von and Jeff had gone all out, buying matching tennis wear in appropriately loud colors. Shaf was decked out brilliantly as well, but with his physique, he could just about pull off anything short of a tutu. I chose to play in a warm up suit that was conservatively put together in a pale blue. Pale seemed to go with my playing style so I thought it was appropriate.

I should also mention at this point that many years ago I made a deal with the Lord. "Dear God, You keep me alive and I promise, I will never expose my legs in public." He has kept up His part of the bargain, so I have no intention of violating my part. As a result, no one has seen my legs as an act of God's grace. Those two sticks of electric whiteness between my trunk and my feet have remained closely guarded, as to not contribute to blindness to those who don't know better than to immediately look away.

My leg coverings included my outfit for the tennis marathon. The other three could look all cool in their short, short, 1979 tennis shorts, but it was long pants for the tall thin weak one.

We gathered at the college's center court at the appointed time that Friday morning. The other three felt that warming up was important, whereas I adopted the philosophy, 'we're going to be playing tennis for the next 24 hours, so I will remain at rest for as long as is allowed by law.'

At 9:50 A.M., Chapel ended in the Main Auditorium and, as we had hoped, a steady stream of students began making their way to the courts. A few students actually cheered for us, but it was later discovered that they thought Ron Von and Jeff were the college tennis team and that Shaf and I were competitors from another school. Oh well. Volunteers were working hard, signing up folks for their monetary donations.

At 9:57 A.M. four proud men strode boldly onto the court and the President of the Bible College offered up a prayer. I was pleased, as I thought it was appropriate that we began the tennis marathon by holding hands and praying. If I was going to survive the next 24 hours, it was going to require supernatural intervention from Heaven above.

God was smiling down to begin with by giving us a picture perfect south Florida day. The sun was shining radiantly, the tall palms surrounding the tennis complex were waving lazily in the light breeze, the temperature was gloriously mild. Even the humidity was on the lower side, so that it would be quite possible that we could get through this endurance contest without completely sweating out our clothes.

The first game of the first set was brisk. I was stunned at how competitive the game became right out of the gate. Like the students watching from the sidelines, I was awed at some of the volleys taking place between Ron Von, Jeff and Shaf.

These guys were good. But the foursome was askew. It was like Bjorn Borg, Jimmy Connors and John McEnroe, joined by Squiggy from *Laverne and Shirley*. This was doubles, so I quickly resorted to the strategy that had won me so many victories when I played on the same team as my wife. *Stay out of the way!*

When 10:55 A.M. arrived, we took our first of 23 breaks we would enjoy over the next full day. Granola bars in green wrappers and bottles of matching green Gatorade had been provided for us during the breaks and I helped myself to a hearty portion of both. Staying out of the way required focus and stamina so I didn't want to wear out too soon.

Shaf and I also used the break to discuss strategy. We had begun with Shaf on the left side of the court and me on the right. That way, he could grab all the shots in the center with his forehand, virtually eliminating the need for my woefully inadequate backhand. But we were still vulnerable on the right sideline. Shaf encouraged me to play closer to the sideline, to which I gladly concurred. As each hour pressed on, I was getting farther and farther to the right.

After a few more hours it was apparent that Ron Von and Jeff had discovered our weak spot—any ball that I had to field. Shaf, being the ultimate competitor did not want to go down without a fight, so he put forth a strategy so extreme, so bizarre, that people are still talking about it today, still in utter disbelief.

"If we're gonna win this, Butter," Shaf said to me at one break, (he loved to call me Butter), "we're gonna have to mix things up."

"Oehemmhkeyy," I said, my mouth full of granola bars.

"Instead of playing side by side, let's play front and back."

Choking on my granola bar, I chugged some Gatorade so I could ask the all-important question. "Who's up front?"

"Me," Shaf replied.

"I like it," I chimed in immediately.

"Good," he said. "You stand behind me and get whatever shots I can't."

I smiled. Knowing the raw competitive nature of my friend Shaf, I knew what he had just said was code for, "Relax. I can take it all from here."

I'm dumb, but I'm not stupid. I surrendered my side slot to Shaf, giving him full reign of the court. I gladly yielded my position to him, knowing he would handle it much better than I ever could have on my own.

Fortunately we made that strategic change early in our marathon. Around noon. So for the next 22 hours I watched some amazing tennis from the best seat in the house. It was like actually being on the court, yet not having to exert oneself in a physical manner. All I had to do was serve when it was my turn and return serve when it was my turn. Once the ball was served, it was all about getting out of the way.

Shaf was a machine, seeming to never tire. Our breaks consisted of him lying face down on the sideline, recharging his batteries with a small season of immoveable rest. I, on the other hand, continued to enjoy granola bars and Gatorade, with the exception of one hour, when it was discovered that I had polished off the entire box and was in need of a student to go fetch more sustenance for the weary warriors.

The longer we played, the thinner the crowd became. As darkness approached our Friday frolic, there were only a handful of curious observers left and by 9:00 P.M. we were by ourselves. Friday night was date night at the college. I guess no one wanted to enjoy the cheap date of watching one guy watch three other guys play tennis.

The night hours were the hardest. No one to cheer you on. No one to replenish the soon to be empty Granola Bar box. It was just the four of us. It was Ron Von and Jeff valiantly trying to put the screws to Shaf. But, he wouldn't give up. He was as awesome under the lights as he was in the spotlight of the sun.

Overnight is a blur to me. I have fuzzy memories of something or other occurring in between Granola Bars and Gatorade. The Granola Bars began tasting like gravel, lightly salted, and the Gatorade was a green mouthwash that I continued to choke down. I remember wanting to lie down, but I knew if I did I would fall fast asleep, not to be awakened till a summer storm might hit a few months from now.

There's that old expression 'the darkest hour is just before the dawn,' and I think whoever said it knew tennis. That 4:00 A.M. and 5:00 A.M. couple of hours were brutal. Especially for Shaf. It was as if he was playing two guys by himself. I really felt for the guy. But, he wanted to win and this was the winning strategy—there was no doubt about it.

The sun made its arrival a few minutes before our 5:55 A.M. break, and the four of us took a brief moment to thank God and to congratulate each other for making it through the night. But it was truly brief, because it was Shaf's serve and he wanted to smoke Ron Von with yet one more ace.

The last few hours of the marathon went along without incident, just like the first 20+ hours went. We were four gentlemen, having a civilized game of lawn tennis. I loved that wording, for in fact I was the greatest gentleman, politely deferring to my partner at every shot. By 9:45 A.M. Saturday morning a small crowd of less than 50 people converged to watch us finish our endurance contest.

At 10:00 A.M., we collapsed into one another's arms, pleased to have done something so noble, yet exhausted to the point of silliness. "Let's keep playing!" Ron Von shouted, as I threw my racket at him with precise aim. We shuffled off the court, found our wives, and found our way back to our respective homes. Sleep deprived, I showered, fell into bed and closed my eyes, knowing two truths would endure:

I wouldn't wake up until Thursday.

I would never be able to face Granola Bars and Gatorade together again.

*     *     *

The dictionary defines a component as 'one of the parts of something, such as a system or mixture: an important piece of something.' In its most basic form, there are only three components to supernatural influence: you, the Holy Spirit, and yielding.

You have the ability to influence simply because you have a pulse and breathe in air. This is what I refer to as *natural influence*. We influence people, for the better or for the worse, simply because we are in their presence.

Moving from natural to supernatural requires the involvement of something or more precisely Someone who is bigger, better and more powerful than we are. Enter the Holy Spirit. God's Spirit can take the everyday, mundane, seemingly insignificant parts of life and give them supernatural power and meaning. He can take a casual comment, as in, *you might like this*, and turn it into a Divine Decree. Of course, this begs the question, how do we move from the natural to the supernatural?

That's the third component—yielding. By giving into God's Spirit, allowing Him to take control of your life in its entirety, you place yourself in the position to allow God total access to do the things He really wants to do.

The Apostle Paul said it best in his letter to the Romans:

> *I urge you therefore, brethren, by the mercies of God,* **to present your bodies** *a living and holy sacrifice, acceptable to God, which is your spiritual service of worship.*
>
> *And do not be conformed to this world, but* **be transformed** *by the renewing of your mind, that you may prove what the will of God is, that which is good and acceptable and perfect.*
>
> —Romans 12:1-2 NASB (emphasis added)

I surrender to God. I yield to Him and He transforms what I say and do into the supernatural work He intended. It is through His Spirit that insignificant conversations become life-altering words. It is through His Spirit that small acts become great deeds, influencing those that are around us.

In many respects, this yielding is the key action of my life. It is the supernatural version of a silly strategy for doubles in tennis. *Stay out of the way!* Allow God's Spirit to work in you by yielding to Him—giving Him the whole tennis court to play as His own. Your job is to stay out of His way, always being available, of course, but mainly watch Him work. I admit, it is a silly strategy in tennis, but it is a profound procedure for life.

You have influence naturally. What we want to get to is moving from natural influence to supernatural influence. The key component is our consistent yielding to the Holy Spirit, being sensitive to the doors of influence that He opens for us.

***Influence moves from natural to supernatural by yielding to His Spirit.***

# CHAPTER 7

# The Consciousness of Everyday Influence

consciousness

con·scious·ness

kon-sh*uh* s-nis

NOUN

1. The condition of being conscious : the normal state of being awake and able to understand what is happening around you.
2. The quality or state of being aware especially of something within oneself.
3. The state or fact of being conscious of an external object, state, or fact.

\*      \*      \*

"Just have a seat down in the Father's Waiting Room, Mr. Butterworth, and we'll let you know when you're baby has arrived."

Some of us are old enough to remember when that was the drill for expectant fathers. No Natural Childbirth—the more unnatural the better. Lamaze sounded like a Japanese crossword puzzle. Breathing exercises were only for swimmers and asthmatics. The closest you could get to your wife and your baby was five hundred yards. Separated by large steel doors, sterilized instruments and nurses and doctors, clad in all white, it was a very different time.

I am old enough to have had that Father's Waiting Room experience. Just once, with our oldest child. When baby number two came along we had transitioned into the Natural Childbirth Era, celebrating all the good that came with it and lamenting all the stuff that used to occur back in olden times.

The year was 1976. For most of us, the highlight of the year was the Fourth of July, when the nation celebrated its 200th Birthday. Of special note was the parade of historic sailing vessels that proudly navigated the waters of New York Harbor. Two-hundred-twenty-four Tall Ships and thousands of small boats cruised up the Hudson. President and Mrs. Ford even attended, giving it still greater gravitas. It was a far cry from *The Era of Good Feeling*. The summer of '76 was right in the middle of what I call *The Era of Trying To Get The Good Feeling Again*. Nixon had been out of office long enough that the Republicans were urging us to forget about it and move on. Carter was seemingly coming out of nowhere, challenging Ford, who was still uncomfortably connected to his predecessor. It was not a fun time to be a government employee.

I would love to tell you that I was politically aware and politically active as a result of the deep love for my country at that time in my life, but it would be pure fiction. I turned 24 the day after New York's Big Boat Parade and the truth is my life centered on my new wife, my new baby and my new avocation. I'll tell you more about my wife and baby in a little bit, but let me tell you about my avocation, since it began years before marriage or parenting entered the picture.

Remember my Dad's one indulgence in his youth? It was playing the saxophone, for he was madly in love with the Big Band sound of the day. So it comes as no surprise that I was handed a musical instrument in elementary school, in the hopes I could realize what Dad never could. "We usually don't start children on the saxophone," Mr. Maio, the music teacher informed my parents. "The clarinet is where we begin and as he masters that instrument, we will move him to the saxophone at your request." As if they needed further persuasion, he left my parents with this musical tidbit: "Clarinet players transition to the saxophone with ease. Saxophone players transition to the clarinet with difficulty."

That settled it. I was playing the clarinet. Every day for almost three years I faithfully put in my thirty minutes of practice. I hated it, but I did it. There didn't seem to be a payoff for playing the clarinet. Nobody thought it was cool, but I did it for Dad.

As was promised, when I entered junior high I was transitioned to the saxophone. Before I left elementary school, I overheard Mr. Maio tell my parents, "We will give him a saxophone next year. But I must be honest and tell you that Billy never really came close to mastering the clarinet. The saxophone will be easier."

I guess I never mastered the sax either, because each year they kept giving me a bigger sax until I was playing the Baritone Saxophone, basically a musical instrument the size of a refrigerator. There weren't a lot of parts written for the Barry Sax, so I was given Tuba parts instead. Thus, rather than intricate musical passages to be mastered, I was playing a lot of Bump, Bump, Bump, Bump—keeping time with quarter notes alongside a jolly group of rotund tuba players.

I still hated it. In desperation, I turned to the golden instrument of the day—the guitar. Asking for one for Christmas, like most children of the mid to late 1960's, I was given a Silvertone guitar, sold exclusively at Sears for the cheapest price of a guitar anywhere.

I didn't hate it. I loved it. Teaching myself to play the three chords all songs of the day included, overnight I was accompanying everyone from Peter, Paul, and Mary, to the Beatles, with *I Am A Rock* and *Hang On Sloopy* in between. It wasn't long before I put a little folk trio together, two guitars and an upright bass. Coffee houses were big at the time, so we learned some folk songs, plus a couple of Christian songs just in case the Coffee House was sponsored by a church. We never hit the big time, but we had a blast.

With my guitar and its trusty three chords, I tried my hand at writing some songs. The trio agreed to sing them and I'm not sure if people liked them, but no one booed, threw fruit or rotten eggs. Encouraged by this lack of violence, I kept on writing.

In 1970, I was off to Bible College in the autumn of the year. I auditioned for a large music group, made the cut and continued in music that entire year. The following year, I put together another group of my own, this one with three guys and three girls, one guitar and one electric bass. Feeling good about my writing, almost every song we did was one of my own compositions. Since these were Bible College years, all the songs I was writing were Christian songs and our group performed almost entirely in churches and church-sponsored youth groups.

One Sunday night, we were unloading our van full of sound equipment at the front entrance of the Bible College, having just returned from a concert at a local church. Still in our 'outfits' (yes, it was back in the day when groups still wore matching attire), an older gentleman, quite nattily dressed, was standing in the lobby and decided to strike up a conversation. "Are you a music group?" asked the man with the silvery white wavy hair.

"Yes," I replied politely.

"What kind of music do you perform?" he continued.

"Actually, I write all the music for this group," I said with youthful, unrestrained, cocky pride.

"Really?" he replied. "My son writes music, too. And he publishes music as well."

"Really?" I answered, now my turn to be curious.

"Yes. Have you ever heard of Zondervan Publishers?"

"Of course," I answered. "They publish John W. Peterson."

"That's right," my new best friend replied. "Let me write down my son's address for you, okay? You should send him three or four of your best songs. Who knows, he may buy 'em and publish them for you."

The kind older man was Jack Wyrtzen, the founder of the worldwide ministry known as *Word of Life*. He had been speaking on campus that night in the chapel. He gave me his son, Don's address. The next morning I sent my four best tunes to Don, care of Zondervan. To my amazement, not too long after, Don sent me a reply letter that included a contract to buy two of the four.

Thrilled, I picked up the phone and called my even newer best friend, Don Wyrtzen. Thanking him for buying the two songs, I launched into a conversation that was ridiculously filled with naiveté. "Now that you've got a couple of my songs, the next thing I want you to do is publish a full book of my songs," I said, as if this was the normal ascension of a musical genius.

"It really doesn't work that way," Don laughed and explained patiently. "Frankly the only person who gets a full book of his music is John Peterson and that's because he writes musicals."

"What's the difference between a book of songs and a musical?" I asked.

"Musicals are songs woven together by a theme. There's usually narration between numbers as well."

"All right," I said, refusing to be discouraged. "I will write you a musical and send it off as soon as it's finished."

"Okay," Don said with another restrained laugh. "If you're serious—make it a musical for teenagers—youth choirs—and we'll take a look at it."

I wrote it.

They bought it.

It came out in the summer of 1976.

Part of their marketing strategy was to publicize premieres throughout the country. There was one in Grand Rapids, the home of Zondervan. (That was a biggy because they flew me up there and as the choir sang, I was seated on the front row next to my musical hero, John W. Peterson!) There was one in Los Angeles and another in Dallas. With me at the Bible College in Miami, south Florida seemed like the natural locale for another premiere.

This one would be different, however. The composer himself would be directing the choir in the Bible College's massive auditorium. The date was set for Saturday evening, August 14th.

It was a muggy south Florida night. I was decked out in a three-piece, all white suit and since it was mid-1970's the suit's lapels were as wide as extra large pizza slices (think John Travolta in *Saturday Night Fever,* yet I was one year ahead of the trend).

My wife told me I looked good, but since we had been married a little over a year at that point, we were still in the phase where you don't get brutally honest with your spouse. I was telling her over and over how good she looked because she really needed to hear it—she was nine months pregnant.

The concert began and I was as excited as I had ever been. The place was full, the choir sounded great. I was in my element. Nothing could possibly go wrong to ruin this new version of *The Era of Good Feeling*.

But then came the Intermission.

Back in the Green Room, I was sitting comfortably with my feet up and my John Travolta jacket hung on the back of the door so as not to wrinkle it. The door behind the jacket suddenly swung open with a sense of urgency all its own. It was my wife. I thought she had come back to congratulate me on the first half of the musical, but she had a different message.

"My water just broke," she announced in strong tones.

"Wow," I responded with incredible empathy.

"That means we need to go to the hospital," she continued. "Now."

What happened next is a moment of which I am not proud. Being all wrapped up in my own little world of music, I replied to her with this awful statement:

"Okay. Let me finish the second half and we'll zip."

She looked at me with a combined expression of pain, disappointment, anger and heartbreak.

And being the fool that I am, I marched back onstage and conducted the second half of my musical.

\*　　　\*　　　\*

Less than two hours later we were at the hospital. The women in the white nurse's uniforms put my wife in a wheel chair and promptly whisked her away to the Labor and Delivery section. Thankfully, she was deemed as not yet ready to deliver so they sent us home and told us to return in the morning. That eased a bit of the humiliation I felt in putting a chorus in front of a child, melody in front of maternity, downbeats in front of delivery.

Bright and early the next morning we were in the car, off to Hollywood Memorial Hospital. Once again they wheel chaired her, but this time they instructed me to head down a darkish corridor to the Father's Waiting Room. I waved goodbye, completely unaware that the Sunday morning wave goodbye would be the last time I would see her until mid-Monday morning.

Once my wife was wheeled away, I navigated the poorly lit hallway and located the Father's Waiting Room. The room was perfectly square, with large vinyl-upholstered furniture that your skin would stick to if it was, for example, August. Even though it was daytime, the lack of windows, coupled with floor lamps with low wattage bulbs gave it a dim look. But it was better than the ice blue flash of light that would strike when a new potential dad would walk in and turn on the overhead fluorescents. The flash would shock us all and immediately the switch was returned to the off position. There was a TV along one wall, but these were the days prior to the cable explosion, and there was not much of interest to a guy on NBC, ABC, or CBS.

The main activities seemed to be reading or smoking. The smokers were not reading and the readers were not smoking. I don't know what that means sociologically, but I found this fascinating, so I pass it along for someone smarter than me to formulate a theory.

I fell into the reader category only to discover that the offerings were quite dismal. I remember sighing as I reminded myself that this was August of 1976 and yet my magazine choices were an issue of *Sports Illustrated* that celebrated the 1972 Perfect Season of the Miami Dolphins, or a *Time* magazine, whose cover story was a look at Nixon's chances in 1968, or a classic issue of *Life* magazine, with the first pictures of Ike since his 1955 heart attack.

This scene has played out in countless old movies and TV shows. Dads sit nervously in the Father's Waiting Room until the moment of glory, when a doctor or nurse victoriously strides through the large steel doors with the new son or daughter wrapped tightly in a blanket, all smiles.

Maybe that's how it played out in the movies, but we had a bit of a different wrinkle. Because the Father's Waiting Room was so far away from the Labor and Delivery section of the hospital, the staff actually installed a pay phone on the wall of the waiting room. When your baby was born, the phone rang. Every man would spring from his seat, all wanting to be the man who answered the phone, believing this would somehow indicate the doctor wanted to speak to him and him alone. Having sat there as long as I did, I saw that dog wouldn't hunt.

The pay phone would ring, we would all jump, Joe Smith would get to the phone first, scream into the phone, "Hello, this is Mr. Smith," only to be greeted by the voice on the other end of the line saying, "Would you please put Mr. Jones on the phone?" At that point Mr. Jones would grab the receiver and receive instructions on where to meet the doctor and the new child. The dads bonded in that ugly little room, so we would congratulate our brother, slap him on the back, and send him off in blissful joy, while we would return to an issue of *Reader's Digest* from 1959.

Soon Sunday became Monday. It was a little after 10 in the morning when the pay phone rang through the dreariness, just as it had so many times before. "Would you put Mr. Butterworth on the phone, please?" Hurtling to the phone, I was given instructions of where to go and I went, after thanking all my new buddies for a great couple of days of male bonding.

Arriving at the large steel doors, I was invited in and directed to look through the glass of the hospital's nursery. There, surrounded by a sea of ugly babies, was the most perfect little angel a man could hope for. I was getting my first look at my new daughter, Joy.

Once I confirmed that she was absolutely healthy in every way imaginable, I asked about her mom. "She's still a little groggy from the anesthesia, but you should be able to see her shortly." I returned to the waiting game, but this time I was surrounded by crying newborns instead of whining men.

When I finally got to see my wife, I asked her to describe the experience to me. "Most of it I don't remember," she admitted. "They knocked me out and the next thing I knew I was waking up with a baby."

The anesthesia worked. The desired result was achieved. A clear absence of awareness.

*       *       *

The birth of my son, Jesse, was the polar opposite of Joy's birth. In the fourteen months between her birth and his birth, the hospital had gotten on board with the whole Natural Childbirth movement.

Mom and Dad eagerly attended the Natural Childbirth classes at the hospital in preparation for what the nurse/instructor laughingly referred to as 'Labor Day.' We practiced breathing exercises that emphasized a four beat rhythm—'he, he, he, who,' with the 'he's' being short breaths and the 'who' being a big one. We learned the importance of choosing a focal point, something like a family photo or a picture of a beautiful meadow—anything that you could look at that would take your mind off the brutal fact that contractions hurt like nothing else you've ever felt before. We were shown a movie where we watched a natural childbirth take place. Later I would comment on how much smiling there was in that movie, in contrast to the lack of smiling I would personally experience through the process.

Eventually, October of 1977 arrived which was the month our second baby was to be born. On a warm Monday afternoon in south Florida, once again water broke. Since I had a lot of meetings that afternoon, I sent her on to the hospital without me, promising to catch up with her later. Are you kidding? After the first child debacle of conducting the second half of the musical, I dropped everything and drove her to the hospital right away. Plus, this was Natural Childbirth, which meant I was going into the Labor room with her.

In shorthand, Natural Childbirth means forget the anesthesia, this is birth with complete awareness. Don't do drugs. Embrace the pain.

Once in our Labor room, we began putting into reality the things we had practiced for all those preceding months. My wife was becoming increasingly more uncomfortable by the minute, and no matter what we did, nothing helped. She was aware of every nuance of pain. At one point, she growled in utter disgust, 'Who did this to me?" With which she would answer herself by her breathing exercises, "He, He, He, Who!" she literally shouted and underscored it by pointing one of her trembling fingers at me.

Another aspect of this birth that differed from the first was the presence of my mother-in-law. She was not allowed in the Labor Room, but she waited nearby for regular updates from me, as I would excuse myself from the contraction action to bring her up to speed.

My mother-in-law was always well meaning, but it often resulted in me getting in trouble. For example, the dear mother-to-be was not allowed to have any food to eat, with the exception of ice chips to chew on. A wimpy substitute at best, my wife soon grew tired of ice chips and was begging for a real bite of something—anything. Of course, as her loving husband, it would have been completely inappropriate for me to eat in her room while she couldn't, so we starved together. It was during one of my update visits to my mother-in-law that she said to me, "You haven't eaten for hours! You must be starving! Here, I just went to the vending machine down the hall and bought a whole package of Oreos. Help yourself, I'll get another package after you go back in the room. I scarfed those Oreos like a man who had spent hours with his pregnant wife in a Labor Room. All six cookies were gone in an instant. I wiped my face of any telltale crumbs, thanked dear Mother, and made my way back in the Labor Room.

Like a woman with a sixth sense, I was not in the room twenty seconds before my wife screamed out, "You've been eating while you were out there! I just knew you couldn't be my teammate. You had to sneak a snack didn't you?"

Before I could dishonestly say no, she quickly added. "Smile at me!" Being dull like last month's razor, I smiled a smile big enough to show her the random black Oreo crumbs that get lodged in between teeth and gums. I was busted. Already in pain beyond belief, her husband conniving to steal a meal behind her back was too much. She broke down. She didn't so much start crying as started to say words I had never heard my wife say. In a moment, the Labor Room sounded more like a meeting of the gang bangers, or the deck of a naval destroyer or a scene from any movie with Joe Pesci in it.

At the next break, I was ready to tell off my mother-in-law, but instead she had information for me. "The baby will be born at 5:00 tonight," she announced boldly.

"How do you know?" I asked.

"I finally figured it out. The doctor's not here, right? He's out playing golf, that what's going on. He will finish and come by the hospital and deliver the baby before he goes home for dinner. Mark my words."

It was ludicrous. I couldn't believe how crazy she was until our son was born at 5:30 that evening, right before the doctor left to go home for dinner.

The birth was unlike the first. The pain was present and there was a total awareness of every pang. Most who read these words will be far more familiar with this sort of childbirth than the ones accompanied by anesthesia. We all have stories either personally or from family or friends about the agony of childbirth. Wags have worked hard to create word pictures to describe it. I recall one comic describing childbirth as akin to pulling your upper lip up over your entire face and stapling it to the back of your head. It would seem that writer had a clear awareness of what was going on.

*       *       *

Awareness or Anesthesia.

Either you're aware or you're not.

Do you want to be more aware? Don't do drugs.

The dictionary defines consciousness as 'the normal state of being awake and able to understand what is happening around you.' It's disciplining yourself to focus on what is going on around you. You have something quite valuable to pass along to those in your immediate circle, so why not make it a constant priority to remain conscious of that privilege? It's the difference between living life by default and living life by intention.

The best way I can encourage you is through two words: *mental focus.* Ask God for the supernatural power to pay attention to how the smallest expression of words or actions can result in the grandest level of impact.

It's not rocket science, but we can use another mode of transportation to be of assistance in our journey. There was a time in our nation when a sign placed where railroad tracks and roadways intersected was truly ubiquitous. Two white long lean signs crossed to form a large X and black letters offered the warning—*Stop, Look and Listen.*

Let the old railroad sign help you by offering three practical steps towards greater consciousness of the influence that is placed all around you: Stop, Look and Listen.

*Stop.*

Busyness is the enemy of consciousness. You and I can get so wrapped up in the routine and the To-Do Lists and the calendar and the hubbub that we lose awareness completely. The Psalmist wrote it this way:

*Cease striving and know that I am God.*

—Psalm 46: 10a NASB

'Be still and know that I am God' is the translation from the old King James. Quietly ask God to make you more conscious of the myriad influential moments that surround you.

*Look.*

Keep your eyes open to all that is around you.

*Therefore, be careful how you walk, not as unwise men, but wise, making the most of your time, because the days are evil.*

—Ephesians 5: 15-16 NASB

Walk carefully, with your eyes wide open. You've asked God to make you more aware, so use your eyes to discover where these opportunities rest. As we shall see, influence is often through actions or circumstances, most often of the subtle variety.

*Listen.*

The people in your life are asking you to influence them; you just need to be listening for it.

*This you know, my beloved brethren. But let everyone be quick to hear, slow to speak and slow to anger.*

–James 1:19 NASB

Talk less. Listen more. That's why you have one mouth and two ears. Do the math. But do it silently, paying attention to the cries from the heart of those close to you.

If you've made it this far in the book, you must be a person committed to being a man or woman of supernatural influence. And you realized this sort of influence most often comes through the little things. Thus, if you want those little things in your life, it is absolutely crucial that you step up your ability to engage in life with greater awareness.

**Influence increases with greater awareness.**

# CHAPTER 8

# The Consistency of Everyday Influence

consistency

con·sis·ten·cy

kən-sĭs'tən-sē

NOUN

1. Agreement or accordance with facts, form, or characteristics previously shown or stated.
2. Agreement or harmony between parts of something complex; compatibility.
3. The state or quality of holding or sticking together and retaining shape.
4. Conformity with previous attitudes, behavior, practice, etc.

\*     \*     \*

Arguably the most demanding event in the summer Olympics is the decathlon.

Ten events, five back to back, each day for two days straight is the greatest demand placed on the human body and spirit in modern day Olympic history. And I am fortunate enough to have known an Olympic decathlete for the last thirty-plus years.

A mutual friend invited us both to join a Friday morning men's group back in 1981. By that time I had moved the family from south Florida to southern California to go to work for the Swindolls (more about that in the next chapter). Five of us men would gather at a local restaurant for a review of what had been going on in our lives, as well as a look at what had been going on in the world, plus a chance to be vulnerable and accountable to one another. It was classic 1980's male bonding.

One wouldn't have known Fred was a decathlete by his personality. Quiet, humble, and far from an attention-getter, Fred was the most silent in our group of five. But physically, one could not overlook him. At six feet, four inches tall, 195 pounds of pure strength, he was an Adonis. If Fred had body fat, he must have stored it in a safety deposit box at the local bank. He was a rock solid mass of muscle, where you found yourself feeling like a schlump even if you just asked him to pass you the salt. Connected to that salt shaker were muscles and veins mingled together to create the arms of a champion.

I loved getting to know Fred. His two sons, Paul and Evan were just the right age to play with my two sons Jesse and Jeffrey when we first met. Play dates had been arranged by their moms and the four of them got along quite well. Since I am as athletic as tile grout, Fred and I were on opposite ends of the athletic spectrum, yet he welcomed me as a friend and we bonded quickly.

Fred's story fascinated me as I forced out bits and pieces so I could put it all together. He had made the United States Olympic team in 1976, so he headed off to Montreal for the games that would be best remembered by another decathlete . . .

. . . Bruce Jenner.

At 26 years of age, Fred was the youngster on the American team so he had his dues to pay as he competed and then watched from a front row seat as Jenner stood on the tallest of the three boxes with the number

'1' on it. Not only did Bruce win the prize of the Olympic Gold Medal, he also won the corresponding ultimate prize, the picture on the front of the Wheaties cereal box. Observing all the hoopla surrounding Jenner, Fred knew that his own career was still maturing athletically and that, God willing, he would achieve his peak performances in four years, in time for the next Olympic Games.

But the political history of the world was not kind to my friend Fred. His hope had come to pass—he truly was in the elite class of decathletes in 1980, as his scores had risen consistently. By 1980 he had achieved an 8390 score in a Decathlon to be listed as the second highest score in United States history. The gold medal in Moscow was his for the taking, had it not been for a "we interrupt your regularly scheduled programming for a special message from the President of the United States" on the first Friday night of January.

On January 4, 1980, a troubled President Jimmy Carter addressed the nation at 9 P.M. Eastern Time from the White House regarding the Soviet invasion of Afghanistan. Within his remarks, he included this tidbit:

*Although the United States would prefer not to withdraw from the Olympic games scheduled in Moscow this summer, the Soviet Union must realize that its continued aggressive actions will endanger both the participation of athletes and the travel to Moscow by spectators who would normally wish to attend the Olympic games.*

It was a foretaste of what was to come. Shortly after the address, the decision was made—the United States would be boycotting the 1980 Summer Olympic Games in Moscow. With that announcement, Fred's dreams were temporarily suspended, if not completely destroyed.

Even though the U.S. team did not participate, it didn't hinder Fred in his training program. A model of discipline, Fred just kept on working out, honing his body and mind for what might be ahead, even though the future was bleak.

It was about this time that I met Fred. We attended the same church and for some reason we were inexplicably drawn to one another—the chiseled athlete and the Pillsbury doughboy—an odd couple indeed.

Fast-forward a few years and all talk of Moscow 1980 had been replaced with the upcoming 1984 Summer Olympics, to be held right here in Los Angeles. Fred was convinced it was far from coincidence that the next summer global event was going to be in his backyard. To make things even more convenient, even the Olympic trials for the United States team were to be held at the Coliseum in Los Angeles as well, just under one hour's drive from Fred's home in Placentia, California.

In the spring of 1984, Fred had a request of the men's group. "I want you to pray for me, guys," he told us with a steely stare in his closely set eyes. "I've prayed about it and I've decided I'm going to participate in the Olympic trials down at the Coliseum. I just don't want to embarrass my family or myself. Most folks don't give me much of a chance because of my age, but I feel like this is what God wants me to do—especially since the venue is so close to home. I can't overlook the facts that I don't have to buy a plane ticket or a hotel room. I can just drive down, do my best, drive home, and sleep in my own bed."

We were all thrilled that Fred had chosen to participate; yet, we knew he would be facing a newer, younger set of competitors. At 34 years of age, one sports reporter for *The Los Angeles Herald-Examiner* took to referring to Fred as 'the dean of American decathletes,' a kind way to allude to his senior status in a young person's sport.

The Men's Group agreed to pray for him, and the stage was set for the events that took place on Thursday and Friday, June 21 and 22.

As if God Himself was attempting to boost Fred's confidence, the first day belonged to my friend.

After the first five events, the 100-meter run, the long jump, the shot put, the high jump, and the 400-meter run, Fred found himself not only competing, but actually leading. As he drove his little Ford Escort back home down the freeway that Thursday evening, he started to allow himself to visualize actually making the team. Once home, he phoned the leader of the men's group, whom in turn called the rest of us to let us know of Fred's success.

Day Two began with the 110-meter hurdles and then moved to the discus, the pole vault, the javelin and the final event, the 1500-meter run. Fred looked good in the hurdles, but he moved from first place to fourth place. Not bad. He was still in the hunt.

It was the next event that took him down. To paraphrase an old adage, 'the devil was in the discus.'

The rules were very straightforward—three throws per person, the best one counts. It was the typical routine for the field events. In his attempt to get back to the top, Fred gave it his all on the first throw, and hurling the plate with all his strength, he fell out of the circle in doing so. That's known as a foul—you have to stay in the circle—so he'd have to choose between his last two throws for his points. On his second throw, it looked just like the first one—including falling out of the circle. Two throws down, only one to go, and no points to show for it at this juncture.

"Fred," his coach took him aside, "you've got to score on this last throw. I know you want to be in first place, but it's more important not to foul out." Nodding in agreement, Fred kept staring down at the ground, as if formulating his own individual plan.

"If I were you," his coach continued, "I'd just stand in the circle and throw it. Don't even run the risk of spinning through the circle. Play it safe. Get some points. You're still in this, man."

As the time came for Fred's final throw, he stood in the circle for a moment before assuming his position at the back of the circle. This meant he was not going to just stand there and throw it. He was going all out, giving it his all.

One of the journalists covering the Trials summarized it this way in his article about Fred:

*. . . on the third, he threw the little platter farther than he ever had in his life. And he fouled. No score in the discus, no chance to make the team.*

Needless to say, Fred was crushed. His Olympic hopes dashed, he robotically moved on to the pole vault, but it was clear to all, his heart was no longer in it. When the vaults were concluded, Fred found his wife Lynn in the stands and told her that he was going to withdraw from the competition and that they could drive home early.

In the little Ford Escort, there was no conversation. It was rush hour, but it wasn't the bumper-to-bumper, fifteen miles per hour traffic crawl that affected them. Fred and Lynn sat in silence, both contemplating the full spectrum of emotional events that occupied the previous 24 hours. In a later reflection on this story, Fred was quoted as saying, "the further we got from the stadium, the worse I felt."

At 5:45 P.M. that Friday evening on the 91 Freeway, the hour-long silence in the Ford Escort was interrupted by Fred's deep baritone voice. "Lynn, you're gonna think I'm nuts, but I have to go back and try to get back in."

They were less than ten miles from home, but Lynn knew better than to offer up any sort of argument. The next off-ramp was somewhere near Cerritos, where Fred exited the 91 Freeway going eastbound and re-entered it, this time heading westbound.

At 6:45 P.M. they pulled into the Coliseum parking lot and Fred jumped out to find a Decathlon official. Miraculously, he found one right away and was allowed to participate in the final heat of the javelin throw. (Unfortunately, there is no record of the conversation that must have ensued with the officials, which must have been quite amusing. "Do you know of any rule that states a participant cannot go home between the eighth and ninth event?" The answer must have been 'no' because Fred was back in it!)

The tenth and final event was the 1500-meter run—always grueling in the most normal of circumstances. One can only imagine how demanding the race must have been for Fred that day. Later he told reporters he really didn't want to run it, but there was a greater reason for it than against it.

His final decathlon was perfectly located in the stadium closest to Hollywood, the movie capital, for the ending was right out of *Chariots of Fire.*

David Osterman, covering the event for *The Orange County Register* put it this way:

> *(Fred finished) with a strong 4:44:44 in the 1500 meters after returning. He was given a standing ovation from the crowd as he came down the stretch for the final time.*
>
> *Fred Dixon had gone out a winner. Not a quitter.*

A standing ovation in the Los Angeles Coliseum!

John Crist, Tim Bright and Jim Wooding had all qualified to make the U.S. team as decathletes. Fifty-three men had begun the process the day before and now there were only 35 left who had actually finished. In one of life's oddities, the press was not circled around Crist, or Bright, or Wooding.

Pens poised over their pads, tape recorders outstretched, the reporters were all huddled around the man who was officially positioned 35th out of 35 finishers. They were all pressed around my friend Fred.

"One of the lessons I try to teach my kids is not to quit," he calmly explained to Frank Lietzke of the *New York Times* that evening. "I was feeling a gnawing anxiety about not finishing the last decathlon of my career. I was afraid my kids would read about it and say, 'You quit your last decathlon.' I want them to be able to follow my example."

Follow his example, indeed.

\*   \*   \*

The example that Fred wanted to communicate to his boys in the language of the decathlete is that life is ten out of ten. Even by going eight out of ten, we leave a mark of influence by the two we dropped.

Remember the Deuteronomy 6 passage?

*You shall teach them diligently to your sons and shall talk of them when you sit in your house and when you walk by the way and when you lie down and when you rise up.*

—Deuteronomy 6:7 NASB

It talks about influencing others when you first get up in the morning and when you retire for the evening at night, as well as when you are inside your house and out in public. To combine the Old Testament with the Decathlon, you are influencing people from the beginning of the 100-meter run through the 1500-meter run; from the highest of hurdles to the devils of the discus. The writer of the New Testament book of Hebrews captures the runner's motif with the following analogy:

*Therefore, since we have so great a cloud of witnesses surrounding us, let us also lay aside every encumbrance and the sin which so easily entangles us, and let us run with endurance the race that is set before us, fixing our eyes on Jesus.*

—Hebrews 12:1-2a NASB

Run the race with endurance. Finish it. And then run the other nine events. Finish them. There are no days off. No extended breaks. Just like you can't do eight of the ten events in the Decathlon and call it complete. We're back to *awareness*. Once we realize there is no 'pause' button in life, the more effective we can be taking advantage of the ever-present 'on' button. There is an advantage in knowing about the consistency of influence.

Fred and I lost contact with each other a few years after the '84 Olympic Trials. Career moves took both of us out of southern California for awhile and we lost touch. But, just a few years ago, I ran into Fred in an airport. We briefly caught up on all our kids and grandkids and then he surprised me by saying that he had recently moved back to Orange County. "I'm back there, too," I replied. One thing led to another and in a full circle move, Fred and I are once again part of a Friday morning men's group that meets to discuss what is going on in our lives, what is going on in the world and a chance to be vulnerable and accountable.

Even more than thirty years later, the truth still remains. Life is more than eight out of ten.

It's all about influence.

It's all about consistency.

***Influence involves every area of your life.***

# CHAPTER 9

# The Circumstances of Everyday Influence

circumstance

cir·cum·stance

sərkəm ˌstans

NOUN

(usually circumstances)

1. A fact or condition connected with or relevant to an event or action.
2. An event or fact that causes or helps to cause something to happen.

\*      \*      \*

I was employed at the radio ministry, *Insight for Living,* or what we affectionately referred to as IFL, back in its early days. They started in 1979 and my hitch went from 1980 through 1987. My title was Director of Counseling Ministries, but my job description could be reduced to one key word—*writing.* I fell in love with writing over my father's Underwood typewriter back in 1960, but I learned the discipline of writing through the never-ending requirements of an ongoing ministry twenty years later.

There were dozens of men and women working in a wide variety of jobs at that time in southern California, in the small town of Fullerton. Thanks to its continued rapid growth, the number of employees was constantly on the upswing. I had been the 33rd employee hired and when I left there was well over one hundred.

One autumn morning in the mid-1980s, we were having an executive staff meeting for vice presidents and directors and we were weighing in on the morale throughout the company. Most of the comments were positive, but one of the vice presidents mentioned that he was observing a possible gap developing between the employees who worked at IFL in the office at desk jobs and the employees who worked in the warehouse, where they engaged in fulfillment activities. To further accent the divide, he reminded us that the offices were housed in one building, while the warehouse was across the street in another building. How could we bridge the gap between these two different types of jobs? We were all on the same team, so there had to be some sort of activity to could unify us.

I don't remember who came up with it, but someone offered an idea that caught on almost instantaneously. It centered on the National Football League. In our little world of Orange County, California, Fantasy Football was a new concept that was just catching on. I admit, I didn't completely understand it all at that time, but it sparked an idea that was simple, yet bonding. "Let's invite everyone at IFL to participate in an IFL Football Poll," it was suggested. "We will give each person who wants to play a list of all the games being played that week in the National Football League. To participate, all you need to do is circle the names of the teams that you think will win. We won't make it complicated with point spreads or anything like that. It will be simple—straight up, win or lose. We will do this for every game of the season. The day after the Super Bowl, we will crown our champion. No money involved. No money to win or lose. First prize is simply knowing that you won it all—and everybody else knowing it as well."

Being a serious fan of the NFL, I thought this was the greatest idea since the invention of the Philly cheese steak. I endorsed it with genuine enthusiasm, praising it for the humanitarian qualities of bringing the employees together, no matter where they were listed on the Organizational Chart, no matter whether they came to work in suit and tie, or blouse and slacks, or jeans and t-shirt. This was an idea whose time had come.

Of course, it didn't hurt that I could justify even more time 'studying' the games that were ahead each week. It was a win-win.

Early each week we were given a single sheet of paper with the games to be played the following Sunday and Monday. It looked like this:

*NFL Week #1*

*Falcons at Saints*
*Browns at Bears*
*Lions at Vikings*
*Oilers at Packers*
*Rams at Cardinals*
*Eagles at Redskins*
*49ers at Bucs*
*Jets at Bills*
*Bengals at Chiefs*
*Colts at Patriots*
*Raiders at Broncos*
*Dolphins at Chargers*
*Steelers at Seahawks*
*Giants at Cowboys*

Making your picks was as simple as circling the name of the winner on each line. Each Friday afternoon our picks were due by 3 P.M. One of the IFL vice presidents was in charge of tabulating everyone's answers and creating the master sheet. By Tuesday morning of the following week, a sheet was passed around that showed each player's position in the most recent total standings. I loved Tuesdays. I was always in the hunt, some weeks standing on top of the pile.

One week, with the best of intentions, I came home from work and decided to start really playing up the IFL Football Poll with the whole family. I can clearly remember thinking, "My kids may be tempted to think that working at a ministry is a boring job with no fun allowed. I'll start telling them about the football poll and in doing so they'll see that being a minister can be an enjoyable calling!"

So I made no apology about regular reports to the family about the office football poll. My excitement level grew with every week of new picks. I was giving it my best shot.

Looking back, it appears that my best shot was too good.

"Can you please stop telling us about the football poll at work?" my kids protested vehemently one night at the dinner table.

I was shocked. What could possibly be the motivation for a comment as cruel as that one? I decided to inquire. "Why don't you want me to talk about the football poll?" I asked. "It's lots of fun and I thought you would like to hear about the fun Daddy has at work."

The kids looked around the table at each other silently, waiting for someone to speak up. After what felt like a lifetime, a brave child finally spoke. "We don't want to hear about your fun at the office. We want to have fun with you here at home."

Question asked and answered.

"Okay," I replied in a bumbling sort of manner, still a bit off balance by their previous comment. "How would you like to have fun with me here at home?" I was bracing myself for answers like more candy and ice cream, or staying up later to watch more television together, or when we go to the park, stay longer, or more wrestling on the Family Room floor. But I didn't expect the answer that they offered.

"We want our own football poll. The Butterworth Family Football Poll!" Their excitement was palpable. It was also contagious.

Thus began the first season of the Butterworth Family Football Poll. We ran it just like I had learned at the office. Straight up, win or lose, no point spread, no money involved, pick every game, crown a champion the Monday after the Super Bowl.

I couldn't believe how excited the kids were. It's important to point out that the kids were quite young back then. How young? Well, let's put it this way—my daughter—the oldest—chose the winning teams based on the colors of their uniforms—that's how young they were.

Since it was within the family, we didn't require them to choose until Saturday night. Faithfully, they would turn in their picks to their old dad, hoping that this week would be the week they broke through and grabbed the lead.

It may surprise you to discover that I didn't win the first year we played the Family Football Poll. That's right, the adult who prided himself in being the Super Fan got blindsided by his daughter, Joy, who took the lead late in the season and never gave it up. And you connected the dots correctly—she's the one who picked the winners based on the colors of the uniforms. I guess it was more about camaraderie than it was about achievement.

In retrospect, creating the Family Football Poll was one of the best ideas we ever came up with. A few years later I had another one of those best ideas to go along with it. I visited the local Trophy Shop and purchased one of those Perpetual Plaques. You know the kind I'm talking about—it's made of wood and it has a large brass plate on the top for the title and then a series of small plates in rows to commemorate the annual winners. *The Butterworth Family NFL Football Champion*, the large brass plate announced. And on the first small plate in the upper left hand corner were the words *Jeffrey 1992-93*.

At the time, I had no idea how influential that family activity would become. It was such a popular pastime in our family life that we still engage in it to this day. I've had to expand the family plaque three times now, just to cover all the people who have won it. These days it's not just the kids and me. It's the kids and their spouses. And more significantly, it's also open to the grandkids. Granted, some have strange ways of making their choices—like choosing based on the colors of the uniforms—but it's all in good fun and getting one's name on the family plaque has taken on legendary status.

*     *     *

*You shall teach them diligently to your sons and shall **talk** of them when you sit in your house and when you walk by the way and when you lie down and when you rise up.*
—Deuteronomy 6:7 NASB (emphasis added)

Returning once again to the Deuteronomy 6 passage, there is a distinction to be made between the two words 'teaching' and 'talking.' The Hebrew word for 'teaching' is the more formal of the two as we have already mention back in Chapter Three. The word translated 'talking' has less to do with words and conversation, and more to do with actions and circumstances. If we were to give it a more modern twist, we might say the text is encouraging us to 'share life together.' It's the dad who not only talks to his kids each night at the dinner table, it's the dad who helps clear the dishes and then goes outside with his kids to shoot hoops at the basket above the garage door on the driveway. It's the co-worker who not only offers occasional advice on how to accomplish a task at work; it's the co-worker who pitches in to help you get it done. It's more than the lecture, it's the living.

Think of influence as a two-sided coin. One side is conversation, the other side is circumstances. Supernatural influence includes both. Most of us are wired in such a way that we do well with one side of the coin, but not the other. We can converse, but we can't join in, or we gladly work side by side, but we do it in utter silence. I stumbled onto this idea of the Family Football Poll and it became one of the most significant circumstances in our family. And there's a bit more of this story that is worth repeating.

These days the poll is a lot more tech friendly, with family members making their choices by email or text or online and I reluctantly admit, we have tried some Fantasy Leagues to make it a bit more challenging now that some of us have grown up. But back in its earlier form, when it was pure and simple, it actually helped me through some tough times.

With five children, I guess we pushed the odds that all would be blissful all the time. We were a very typical family that included good behavior, not-so-good behavior and even a touch of rebellion. One of my sons (and I will keep him unidentified) went through a period of life in his late teens where he could be best described as an angry young man. Granted, he had good reason to be angry. His mom and dad had divorced, leaving him weighed down with an extra backpack of tough questions, on top of the normal burdens a teenager must bear.

The manner in which he expressed his anger towards me was to stop talking to me.

He went off to college and since it was nowhere near home, it felt like our communication had completely ceased. I would do my best to attempt to connect with him, but it all seemed to fall on deaf ears. I was crushed. I tried to understand, but I couldn't shake the blame of it all. I felt that I had let my son down and it appeared there was no way to mend that rip in the fabric of our once whole relationship.

And then came autumn.

After what seemed like many long weeks of no communication with my son, it was now NFL football season. That meant that every Saturday night, without fail, he would have to call me on the phone in order to give me his picks for the week. Thank God it was before the days of email and text. I could actually hear my son's voice on the other end of the line.

Most Saturdays he would be quite disciplined. "Hi, Son!" I would say cheerily as he listened on the other end of the line. His response was quite mechanical. In an unexcited monotone he would reply, "I'll take the Rams, the Dolphins, the Patriots, the Cowboys, the Lions, the Seahawks, the Eagles, the Cardinals, the Steelers, the Broncos, the Colts, the Bears, the Chargers and the Packers." Once he had given me his picks he would abruptly end the phone conversation. "See ya," he'd say as the line went dead.

But, thank God, there were those occasional slip ups, when he would give me his picks and actually talk with me, if only for a few minutes before he realized what he was doing and then resort to the quick hang up.

"How's it going?" I would ask after his picks had been recorded.

"Okay," he'd reply, still without a hint of emotion. "I've got some hard classes this semester, so it's kinda rough."

"Do you need anything?"

"Nope," he'd say, suddenly realizing he was actually conversing with me. "I'm fine. Gotta go."

And with that, he would hang up.

I don't know what that story means to you, but my guess is if you have ever had a loss of communication with a family member, you know that those few minutes each week on the phone were *golden*. It was the high point of the week for me.

There's nothing necessarily supernatural about an NFL Football Poll—it's a natural circumstance in life. But, it certainly can move into that supernatural category. It's up to you. I've had people who have heard me tell this story begin a football poll of their own and send me photos of what they chose as their family trophy. Many choose a plaque like ours, but still others get creative. One guy bought a real football helmet from his hometown pro team. Whoever wins that year gets to display the helmet in his or her choice location and they also get to autograph the helmet with a sharpie. Another guy sent me a photo of a trophy he found that looks like the typical trophy of days gone by, except that up top, where the old ones have the bowler or the golfer or the baseball, this one has an old man sitting in a reclined recliner. It's the Couch Potato Trophy and everyone in his family covets it.

The NFL Football Poll is an illustration of a circumstance in our life. One of the dictionary definitions for the word 'circumstance' is 'an event that causes something to happen.'

Like doing life together.

It's one of the Circumstances of Influence.

***Influence occurs not only by my words but also by my actions.***

# CHAPTER 10

# The Caring of Everyday Influence

caring

car·ing

ˈkɛərɪŋ

VERB

Feeling or showing care and compassion.

\*     \*     \*

The air was warm, thick and humid on the final day of August in 1999. After a full day of travel, I was getting all settled into my room at the historic Grove Park Inn located in Asheville, North Carolina, where I was scheduled to speak the following morning to the North Carolina Association of Certified Public Accountants. My assigned subject was *How To Get Along With Almost Any Client, Customer or Co-worker.* Having addressed this group on previous occasions, I knew we would be in for an enjoyable morning together.

Not only was I excited to be back with a group of friends, I was thrilled to be located in this particular venue. The Grove Park Inn offered the pleasant aroma of history, not to be confused with a musty smell that one might find offensive. William Jennings Bryan had delivered the Keynote Address at the hotel's grand opening in 1913. Virtually every U.S. President from William Howard Taft forward had stayed in the granite fortress. And of particular interest to me, the renowned writer, F. Scott Fitzgerald took a room at the Grove Park Inn for two years while his wife was institutionalized in a nearby Asheville asylum. He continued his writing throughout the ordeal and to this day, room 441 is preserved as it was maintained in the 1930's, as a tribute to the extended stay of their famous guest.

I ordered a light dinner from room service and decided to do a little exploring while waiting the hour I was told it would take to deliver the food to my room. The CPA's did me the favor of putting me in the newer wing of the hotel, so I decided to snoop around the older section, hoping to find Fitzgerald's room for a quick peek at greatness.

My ability to discern direction is seriously disabled. To call me directionally challenged is to take getting lost to new and greater depths. Not knowing where I am located happens to me when I drive, when I walk, actually any form of movement that would require me to comprehend where I'm going and being in charge of said movement.

Thus, my little excursion to find room 441 turned into a field trip that almost required overnight arrangements in the dark hallways I traversed. As an act of God's grace, I did finally find room 441, but regrettably it was already locked up for the evening, with the cheery little sign hanging off the doorknob, inviting me to return tomorrow for a look inside.

Getting back to my room was as ugly as finding my way to F. Scott's. To make lemonade out of lemons, I should note that when one is lost in a building, one gets to see the vast majority of the building, at least the areas that are open to the public. Once the thorough inspection of the hotel was accomplished, I found my way back to my room, called room service yet again, and had my dinner delivered, after a scolding about how it had been delivered once already, but no one was there to receive it.

Having an evening of cold food and closed doors, I decided to place a call to Newport Beach, California for a bit of cheering up. My spirits lifted as I chatted with the woman who would become my wife in twelve short days. Yes, that meant our wedding day was September 11th, but this was 1999, two years before the tragedy that would change the way we all view that date.

After Kathi and I chatted for a bit, she bade me good night and I rolled over to sleep soundly. The alarm blared hours later to announce a brilliant sunrise on a day that promised to be cooler and less humid than its predecessor. Once I was ready for public consumption, I found my way to the Ballroom, which means I left three times earlier than it would take for a non-directionally challenged person to find the Ballroom. I knew I had seen it last night in my extensive tour, but I just wasn't sure where it was located, exactly.

The speech went off without a hitch. The CPA's were an enthusiastic audience. (I know many think of CPA's as some of the more reserved creatures on the planet, but if you can get them away from their desk and send them to a convention, they are born again into party animals.) I thanked them for their kindness and made my way back up to my room.

Upon entering the room, the small red light on the room phone was blinking, meaning I had a message. Lifting the receiver, I dialed the Front Desk and was told that one of Kathi's friends had called and that it was very important that I call back immediately.

"There's something wrong with Kathi's back," her friend explained once I connected with her. "We've got her here in the emergency room right now and I'll call you when we know more."

"Can I talk with her?" I asked.

"No. Not right now. She's in with the doctors and we'll let you know as soon as we can."

I hung up the phone in a dazed condition. What had happened? Is she going to be okay? It's her back? Did she fall down? Was it all the stress of the wedding plans? I decided no matter what it was, I was more needed in California than North Carolina, so I began packing up and making my way to the Asheville airport.

By the time I was on the ground of the West Coast, Kathi was home, resting at her condo. "I have a few herniated discs in my back," she explained to me. "I'm on some pretty heavy duty drugs, but they think I'm going to be okay."

"Think?" I repeated.

"No one knows anything for sure at this point," she said.

"Can we still get married next Saturday?" I asked.

"Absolutely," she answered, her smile melting away all my concerns.

For the next couple of days, Kath spent most of the hours either in bed or on the sofa, assisted by the proper amount of pain medication.

In an attempt to be helpful, I checked Kathi's answering machine. "If we don't get this last pre-marital counseling session in, we're not going to be able to have the wedding ceremony in the Chapel. You have to have three counseling sessions—it's church policy."

The voice on the phone's answering machine was our friend, Bill Flanagan, affectionately known as Flan. He was in charge of the counseling sessions Kathi and I were receiving in order to allow acceptance for a wedding in the beautiful Chapel of St. Andrews Presbyterian Church. We had first contacted Flan back in the spring and he happily agreed to perform our ceremony. The biggest adjustment he would have to make concerned the fact that we were going to provide him with a bit of assistance. That's code for, we were going to have *three* ministers officiating at our wedding. If one was good, three would be great. At least that's the way we viewed it.

Kathi had become acquainted with Flan almost ten years before when she attended the Divorce Recovery Classes that were run by him at St. Andrews. A pioneer in that field, Flan had helped hundreds, maybe thousands of people adjust to the single again status, guiding the program with compassion and wisdom.

Up to this point, we had willingly complied with the guidelines set forth by St. Andrews in order to have the ceremony in their Chapel.

By having Flan officiating, we complied with the rule that stated a St. Andrews minister must officiate. The first two counseling sessions were helpful in gaining additional insights into our strengths, weaknesses, similarities and differences in our new relationship.

"The final counseling session will be a lot different than these first two," Flan explained to us that night in his office at the end of Session Two. "We will turn our attention to the Wedding Ceremony itself. We'll discuss all the elements and the order of the service and the participants and all the information we'll need to digest in order to insure a Wedding Ceremony that goes off without a hitch."

Our intention had been to visit Flan for our final counseling session about two weeks before the wedding. But busyness prevailed and then the back injury occurred.

When I returned the phone call to Flan, I tried to be as informative as I could be, but the last thing we wanted to hear was that the wedding would need to be postponed.

"How are you, Bill?" Flan asked.

"I'm fine, but I'm afraid Kathi is in a bad way right now," I replied.

"What's happened?" he asked, genuinely concerned.

I explained the story of the herniated discs and followed it with a big favor. "Flan, I know we need to do this final counseling session and Kath and I are willing to do it, but I'm wondering if, instead of meeting in your office, would you consider coming over to her condo and meeting us there? That way, Kath can stay on the sofa where she's much more comfortable."

"That wouldn't be a problem at all," Flan agreed immediately. "Give me the address and I'll be there. Would tomorrow afternoon around 3:00 P.M. work?"

"Perfect," I answered. "See you tomorrow."

I hung up, shared the good news with Kath and returned to anything a guy could do to help his bride prepare her wedding day. Basically, I watched a Dodger game.

The next afternoon, around 2:55, the Reverend William Flanagan knocked on the door of Kathi's condo. "Stay there, I'll get it!" I joked, as if Kathi were going to jump off the couch and race me to the door.

"Thank you," she replied, with that 'you're so silly' look on her face.

Flan entered the condo and I directed him to an armchair that faced the couch where Kathi was reclining. I had moved one of the dining room chairs over next to the sofa so I could sit near her.

Flan asked my bride-to-be how she was feeling and Kath went into a review of the last few days of her life. She recounted tales of emergency rooms, poking and prodding, meds to take orally, even an epidural, a pain reliever that comes in a needle the size of the one in Seattle. There was no mistaking that she had been through quite an ordeal.

As a loving shepherd, Flan was compassionate as he listened to Kathi describe her days. His face was a full one, and his cheeks made him appear almost cherubic. His kind eyes communicated understanding and his nodding head said he could relate to every ounce of discomfort. No wonder Kathi loved this guy and wanted him to officiate at the ceremony.

"Without trying to be indelicate," Flan said as he adjusted his posture in the armchair, "I'd like to change the subject and finalize a few details about the ceremony itself. Saturday will be here before we know it and it's important that the three of us be on the same page."

With that said, we launched into an extended discussion of bridesmaids, groomsmen, songs and soloists, Scriptures and vows. From there we went to Pastoral prayers, the lighting of the Unity Candle, Processional, Recessional, floral arrangements and guest books, seating charts for families, and what to do with unruly children.

Then Flan turned his attention to the rehearsal that would occur the evening before our Wedding Day. We discussed who would run the rehearsal, how long it would take, what would and would not be accomplished and what time to tell the restaurant to prepare the rehearsal dinner.

There were so many details to discuss, I was exhausted by the time Flan began to conclude this session. Maybe what happened next was because I was tired. Perhaps it was because I wanted to lighten the stress that was hanging over the condo like a cloud cover. Or it could have been that I'm just a fun-loving guy who can't resist a little craziness in the midst of situations where others would see it as completely inappropriate.

As I had sat and listened to Flan go over the minutia of the blessed event, I found myself daydreaming a tad and thinking to myself, "He is so kind, so caring, so delightful—he is the perfect straight man for a funny guy to use to set up his punch-lines." I know other guys like this—the consummate straight man—and I treat them with the same love and respect that I extended that afternoon to Flan.

I waited for the right moment and it eventually arrived. "I believe that is all the data I need to discuss about this coming weekend," Flan said as he reviewed a pile of paper work inside his large black leather folder. Closing it, he asked, "Do either of you two have any questions?"

Looking over at Kath, it appeared that she was satisfied with all that had been discussed, so I took advantage of the moment. "Flan, you've been incredibly sympathetic to our plight here and I just want to thank you for being so willing to work with us," I began.

"Well, you're welcome," Flan responded with his contagious warm and engaging smile.

"You know," I continued, baiting the hook as it were, "Kathi and I are both very concerned about her health and how it relates to the ceremony."

"I understand and concur," Flan answered.

"Of particular concern to me is Kathi's ability to walk down the aisle," I pressed on.

Flan picked up on it immediately and took the bait. "I don't want either of you two to worry about it," he consoled. "I can't even remember how many weddings I've done where we had the Bride come down the aisle in a wheel chair."

"A wheel chair?" I repeated for emphasis.

"That's right," Flan beamed and nodded enthusiastically.

"Weeelllll . . ." I began my big moment, "as I mentioned to you on the phone, Kathi is not able to stand and walk without major discomfort. But the same applies for sitting. We are not going to be able to roll her down in a wheel chair on Saturday."

"Hmmm," Flan fretted aloud.

"I can see the concern on your face, my friend," now my turn to console Flan. "I've already given this some serious consideration and I have a plan that I know you'll agree with and will be willing to endorse."

"You do?" Flan said with a degree of curiosity coupled with gloom.

"Yes," I said with enthusiasm. "I have made some calls around town and I've got it all set up that if we need to, we will be able to bring Kathi down the aisle on a *hospital gurney*."

"What?" Flan's jaw dropped as he said it.

"Relax, relax," I said, with the joke only beginning to unfold. "I can see by the expression on your face how shocked you are that I would bring my bride down on a gurney."

Flan looked as if he was beginning to ease up his tense posture.

"It's not right for a bride to be all alone on a gurney in the front of the church," I continued.

Flan's right eyebrow raised itself into a curious expression.

"So don't worry, Flan," I reassured. "I have called all over town and if Kathi needs to be on a gurney, I have secured enough of them for the entire wedding party —all twelve of us—to be on gurneys as well. She will not feel out of place with all of us in the same position."

The usually quiet, reserved Presbyterian Pastor, morphed into the polar opposite, a Pentecostal Preacher. Jumping to his feet, raising both arms in the air, while waving his hands as a good Charismatic might, he bellowed, "We're gonna pray for this lady right now! We're gonna ask God to heal her! Dear Lord, give her the strength to walk down the aisle this Saturday!"

Regaining his composure, Flan once again took his seat and waited to catch his breath. Meanwhile I glanced over at Kath, arrogantly assuming she would be in uncontrollable laughter at what I had just accomplished with her friend.

She was not amused.

I braced myself for the scolding of my life. She had every right to lay into me big time. But she didn't. Turning to Flan, she said, "Bill is having a little fun with you, Flan. He's not going to march me down the aisle on a gurney and he's not going to have the front of the Chapel lined up with twelve of them. He's just kidding around."

At that moment, as I looked at her, all I could think of was the lesson we had learned earlier in our relationship about how we all *choose* to love people. What I viewed as high comedy, Kathi and Flan viewed from a different perspective. I realized it violated the two cardinal rules I had tried to teach my kids about humor—it's all about timing and appropriateness—and I had failed at both.

Yet Kathi chose to love me. She was willing to look outside her own skin and unselfishly come to my rescue. "Bill's sorry for misleading you, aren't you, Bill?" Kathi said to Flan, leading me to the chance to apologize.

"Yes, I'm sorry, Flan," I said. "That was a bad joke at your expense. Would you please forgive me?"

Flan nodded as the color began to reappear in his cheeks and the smile returned to his eyes. "Yes," he replied. "It was all in good fun." And Flan couldn't resist looking directly at Kath and stating, "You must really love this guy!"

\*       \*       \*

Supernatural influence cannot occur if we're living a selfish life. It's doubtful that even a positive influence can result. We have to move out of our self-centered lives to a life of unselfish caring. It's what the Bible reduces to the simple, four-letter word *love*. Jesus forcefully drove home this truth to His disciples, the night before He was crucified.

*"A new commandment I give to you, that you love one another, even as I have loved you, that you also love one another. By this all men will know that you are My disciples, if you have love for one another."*
—John 13:34-35 NASB

Clearly the Apostle John got the message, for he repeated it in his later epistle:

*Beloved, let us love one another, for love is from God; and everyone who loves is born of God and knows God.*
—I John 4:7 NASB

As simple as the message is, what the world needs now, is love, sweet love. Jesus said it—you and I know it. We have to discipline ourselves to break out of our ego-centric modes and reach out in love to those that are around us, choosing to love the people who frequent our lives. Kathi did it and so can the rest of us.

Just a few days later, on Saturday September 11th, 1999, this beautiful woman who was the personification of unselfish love became my wife. I am delighted to report that she marched down the aisle under her own power, no chairs or gurneys necessary.

One might call it the power of love.

**Influence is a natural extension of my love.**

# CHAPTER 11

# The Companions of Everyday Influence

companion

com·pan·ion

kəm'panyən

NOUN

1. A person with whom one spends a lot of time or with whom one travels.
2. A person who shares the experiences of another.

\*       \*       \*

As a person who grew up on the East Coast, the calendar moving from August to September usually marked the conclusion of summer and the commencement of autumn. Sure, there were occasional hot Septembers, which my white, Anglo-Saxon, Protestant parents used to describe as 'Indian Summers,' but overall September meant cooler temperatures, sweatshirts, football and the ubiquitous leaves of many colors.

So it came as a shock to my system when I moved from the East Coast to the West Coast and I experienced my first California September. The first of the month on my first September in Orange County found me unpacking an old, faded, well- worn sweatshirt, a favorite of mine since college days, along with a couple of long-sleeved plaid flannel shirts, just in case the chill was too much. Boy, was I in for a surprise.

September is merely an extension of summer in southern California. There are many years on the southern California coast where we don't really feel summer's arrival until well into July, due to a phenomenon known as 'June Gloom.' So it's not necessarily a long summer, but more aptly a delayed summer. Labor Day used to mean fall is here; now it means fall is only four to six weeks away. My first sweaty September was a foretaste of what I have now experienced for well over thirty Septembers. It's a toasty set of thirty days.

September of 1999 was no exception. For almost twenty years at that point I had long learned that the sweatshirts could stay in the back of the closet underneath the pile of golf shirts that were more appropriate for the day at hand. On the tenth day of that month I picked out one of my nicer golf shirts to wear—the navy blue one with the bold yellow stripes—because I was set to meet some very special people that day and I didn't want to look like a schlump. A very special appointment had been pre-arranged for noon at the Newport Beach Marriott Hotel across the street from Fashion Island, one of the most glamorous shopping malls in the world. It was a lunch meeting with ten other guys, so I laughed at the thought of us being across the street from Fashion Island. It just might be the dictionary definition for juxtaposition.

All ten of these guys were extremely important people in my life, but to my recollection, I never had all ten of them together in the same place. But there was a reason for this collection of friends at this time. We were gathered to celebrate a wedding—my wedding—and this was my seemingly boring way to enjoy a bachelor party. I know, bachelor parties are where guys go wild and crazy and that thought had not escaped my thinking, so I had decided in advance that even though it was a lunch, I was going to shoot off the chart and actually order a dessert. How's that for pushing the envelope?

As the guys arrived there were plenty of handshakes, back slaps and awkward guy hugs. Some of these guys were to be groomsmen in my wedding party; others were simply attending the wedding in support of their buddy. I was thrilled that all of them were there. Once all ten were gathered in the lobby, we made our way to a private room where we could eat and talk and laugh and shout at any volume we desired.

There were times when we were all conversing about the same topic, ten men talking one by one while the rest of us listened attentively. There were other times where the table conversation divided itself up into four or five separate conversations with two or three drawn together by their seating proximity. I tapped my water glass with my butter knife, made a short speech in thanksgiving to each and every one of them for being with me on this special occasion and I handed them each a gift from my heart. It was a Montblanc Fountain Pen with their initials engraved in gold on the side. On my budget, it was a tad expensive, but it was a fraction of what each of these ten men brought to my life over the years we had known one another.

Most of us ordered sandwiches or burgers. The alluring aroma of the accompanying French fries surrounded our table with a blanket of unity, the smell of solidarity, a singular commitment from each of us to individually do what we could to raise our cholesterol. Foolishly, one friend attempted to order a side salad, but observing the peer pressure created at this table of testosterone, thought better of it.

One of the special moments around the table still amazes me to this day. If it were a movie, it would be the part where the outside edges of the screen would get fuzzy and seemingly time would stand still. It would be the flashback montage, a warm recollection of each man in attendance. How I was able to do that in real time, without appearing to be an uncaring host still befuddles me. But it happened. I was able to allow my eyes to wander around that table and focus on my friends, one by one.

Dressed in his floral aloha shirt, my Best Man, Joe was seated about midway down the left side of the table and he was one of the happiest guys at the table. Every time our eyes would meet during lunch that day, he would give me a knowing wink that was his way of saying, "It's all worked out, Bill. God has taken good care of you."

I thought back to the history I shared with Joe. When my life fell apart due to my divorce, my initial strategy was a typical one, especially for a male. I tried to keep my pain a secret. I had honestly convinced myself that no one would ever need to know that I was single again. By keeping people at arm's length, I could go on with my life and avoid those painfully awkward conversations about how I got to the bottom of life's graph paper and what I was going to do to climb my way back up.

Secrecy was silliness. It was impossible to make it work. One of the first guys I decided to open up to was Joe. Our family was living in northern California at the time and as was our custom, each summer we would put the five kids in the van and drive to southern California for a vacation that was wrapped around a visit to Disneyland. We observed this tradition religiously, like Bowl Games on New Year's and chocolate eggs on Easter. When my marriage ended, however, it was not a wise time to be out on the road giving presentations, so I cancelled all my speaking gigs and decided to stay home in order to heal up. It was a good decision in every way but one. I was no longer making any money.

As the bills piled up, the summer was approaching. I deftly danced around the issue of Disneyland with the kids every time it came up for discussion. My head knew we couldn't afford it. My heart wanted to take them anyway and perhaps gain entrance into the Magic Kingdom by applying the old expression 'storming the gates.'

In God's providence, one of the last speaking engagements I took before getting off the road was a speech to the upper management team at Knott's Berry Farm. When my presentation had concluded, they handed me an envelope with my check in it, along with an unexpected act of kindness—six passes to their amusement park. Those free tickets allowed us to continue our annual vacation to southern California. Granted, we wouldn't be able to go to Disneyland, but we'd simply substitute Knott's in its place.

I phoned Joe right before we left to make the eight-hour drive down to Anaheim. "We'll be at the Howard Johnsons right off the 5 freeway," I told him. "We're going to Knott's Berry Farm all day Thursday. Why don't you come over to the hotel on Thursday night and we'll catch up a bit." Joe agreed to meet me at the appointed time and location. As I drove that elongated stretch of California highway, I had plenty of time to think. I quickly came to the conclusion that there was no way I could tell Joe about the brokenness in my life without breaking down and crying. Desperately wanting to maintain a slice of my manhood, I decided I would meet Joe out by the hotel's swimming pool. I would instruct the kids to dive into the pool cannonball style so that Joe and I would constantly be getting wet from the big splashes. In that way no one would know what was pool water and what were tears.

Joe arrived, we hugged and he immediately could sense that something was wrong. "Where's your better half?" he innocently inquired.

"Let's go out by the pool so the kids can swim and I'll give you the answer to that question," I replied. Once seated poolside, the cannonballs commenced, the story unfolded and the tears flowed.

"Does anyone else know about this?" Joe asked.

"Ed does," I answered (more about Ed will be forthcoming). "Other than him, it's just you."

"Does Mike know?" he prodded, referring to a close friend of ours.

"No. Just Ed and you."

"We need to let Mike know," Joe insisted.

"Joe, there are lots of people we need to let know, but for right now I just need someone like you." Joe nodded, leaned forward on the poolside beach chair and listened as I spilled my guts.

We ended our evening confessional well into the darkness that night and as Joe was leaving, he turned and said, "If it's okay with you, I'll be back tomorrow. We'll talk some more."

I nodded in silent appreciation while I rounded up my kids and got them back into the hotel room to get ready for bed.

The pounding on the hotel room door the next morning woke me with a start. I had tossed and turned most of the night and when sleep finally arrived, it was fitful at best. Now with this pounding sound, I wasn't even certain where I was. Grabbing my glasses, I checked my watch—7:30 A.M. Rubbing the sleep from my eyes, I realized I wasn't home and that the beating sound was coming from our own hotel room door. Stumbling over five young bodies strewn all over our room, I got to the door and opened it to view a very big surprise.

"Hi Bill, I hope I didn't wake you." I had thought it would be Joe. It wasn't. It was Mike. "Joe called me last night and told me what was going on. I got here as fast as I could."

"Mike—" I said aloud, before my voice tightened up as tears filled my eyes. He had grabbed the first flight to Orange County he could get from his home far, far away in Omaha, Nebraska.

"A guy going through what you're going through shouldn't be alone at a time like this," he shared wisely and compassionately. "By the way, I brought someone else with me," Mike added, standing aside from the doorway as Joe stepped in behind him, grinning ear to ear.

"I don't want to get in the way of your kid's vacation, but I did want to spend some time with you. Have your kids been to Disneyland this trip?"

I shook my head no.

"If you'd allow me, I'd like to buy your kids tickets to Disneyland," Mike went on. "Two of Joe's kids, Jeff and Jenny will go with them to keep an eye on them, so there will be no need to worry. Then Joe and you and me can have all day to be together to do whatever we want."

By that time the kids were awake, witnessing how amazing my friends truly are. Of course, since I was an emotional train wreck, I was crying like a baby. God, through my friends, was providing the Disneyland trip my kids wanted, in spite of my lack of funds. And He was offering me two men to lean on—two men in whom I had deep respect and trust.

When my brain refocused on the table of guys at that Marriott Hotel, I realized that the summer vacation I was daydreaming about was more than six years ago. But now, at my bachelor party Joe was still seated on the left side of the table towards the center, and Mike, in a dark blue golf shirt, was two guys down from him, near the other end.

On the opposite end of the table—right side, close to me, was my friend, Ron. I can't think of Joe and Mike without thinking of Ron. The four of us began a golf foursome over 25 years ago that is still alive and kicking to this day. Of course, we all live in different places so our golf game is, in reality, an annual event. It's a long weekend in the winter, to allow those in the snow to experience some January sunshine. We've named our foursome something easy to remember—the FAHARI COMB Society. It's an acronym for Fishing And Hunting And Roughing It, Camping Out, Male Bonding. Since we don't hunt, fish, or camp out, the sarcasm just felt like the right thing to do.

The four of us have helped each other in a variety of ways through the years. Golf is just a cover for the real business at hand. We talk. We confide in each other. We pray for each other. We are there for each other. Whether it's divorce, or a faltering business, or a wayward child or health issues, or a battle with pride, we've all taken turns in support of one another.

Over the years, Ron has become my go-to guy when it comes to all things techy. Too many times to count, I have been on the phone with him at his home in Tacoma, Washington, as he unselfishly walks me through why my computer won't boot up or printer won't print or cell phone won't cell. Seated at our table that Friday afternoon, he too was all smiles. These three guys had walked me through the war zone and saw me through to the other side, where my beautiful wife-to-be was waiting for us to exchange our vows the very next day.

As was mentioned earlier, when it came to the actual wedding ceremony, Kathi and I didn't want to leave anything to chance, so we followed this logic: If one minister can preside over a wedding and make it legal, imagine the deeper strength we would forge by having *three* ministers marry us. That thought came to my mind as I stole a bite of my fries and burger while looking directly across the table from Ron to see my dear friend Ed.

In his white, short-sleeved button down shirt, khakis and his super-Preppy, impeccably preserved, brown and beige saddle shoes, Ed was at the luncheon not only as my friend, but also as one of the officiating pastors. Ed and I go way back. His was the first friendship I made when I moved to southern California. We worked together at *Insight for Living* and we used to carpool together to and from work. He never drove to work the same way twice, so every day was an adventure. We logged a lot of miles together and a lot of time together.

To give you an idea of how close we were, in the mid-1980's Ed felt called to take the pastorate of a church in northern California and just a few short years later our family moved to the same small town so we could continue our friendship with this amazing man. Ed had made a great effort to be at this luncheon and at our wedding. There was so much going on in his life at that time, but he somehow managed to get to our event. As I looked at him, he too was smiling. His face looked thinner than I remembered and the dark circles around his eyes gave away the intense fatigue he was experiencing. A few years later Ed would pass away, having lived an influential life that was just too darn short.

Between Joe and Mike sat my friend Bob. He was sporting the most unique outfit of the afternoon. Over top of his long-sleeved, blue, button down Oxford shirt, was a black short-sleeved t-shirt, with a large red circle painted on his chest. Within the red circle were the words *The Strand Bookstore, New York City, Thirteen Miles of Books*. Behind those silver framed glasses, Bob's eyes were dancing, perfectly accompanying his wide smile.

Bob and I met when we both lived and worked together in southern California. His time on the West Coast would be short, and he eventually returned to his home of many years, just outside the wonderful city of Boston. Bob and I had a love for many of the same things, but the most significant was our shared affection for old and used books. For many years in a row, Bob and I would meet up somewhere, rent a car, and visit as many used bookshops as we could in the allotted time. With him living in the Boston area, I loved to come east, especially in the fall, so we could check out the book inventories in states like Vermont, and New Hampshire and even cities like Boston and New York City. So when he showed up in his *Strand* t-shirt, I couldn't help but grin from ear to ear, reminiscing about our used book excursion from several years ago back in the Big Apple.

I silently thanked God for those book trips, because there was much more to them than just perusing shelves of tomes. Bob and I talked; in some ways unlike I talked to any other guy. Being so easy to open up with, I found myself sharing what I would normally keep to myself. And of course, I was always glad I did, for his counsel was good and powerful. The Lord gave me many answers to my many questions through long discussions with my good friend Bob.

Another bite of burger, with my thoughts still on good counsel and good friends, my eyes darted from one side of table to the other and there, sitting directly across from Bob was my friend Ken. One more of the three officiating ministers, Ken and his wife, Mari, were not only friends, they were my unofficial therapists through all sorts of real, unreal and not real emotional traumas.

I first met Ken when he booked me to speak at the Mount Hermon Conference Center where he worked. He would continue to do so many times throughout our friendship and it was at these retreats where I would get some alone time with he and his wife. Shortly after I had the poolside/hotel room encounter with Joe and Mike down in Anaheim, I knew I needed to start some counseling and I also knew Ken and Mari would know exactly whom I should see. Still an emotional basket case, pride and stupidity teamed up to create a foolish conclusion in my head that only 'crazy people' see counselors. So, I made up a story that is the most unoriginal story ever conceived.

"I have *a friend* back in my hometown who is in need of some counseling," I began my fiction during a long walk the three of us took one cool, overcast afternoon.

"A *friend?*" Ken replied.

"Yes, a *friend,*" I emphasized, while averting my eyes from his glance.

"Tell me about him," Mari inquired.

"Well," I continued, "he's going through a rough time in his life due to divorce. He's got a boatload of kids who he fears are getting all messed up by the broken home. He's a good guy, but he really needs to talk some things through." I had woven such a tangled tale that I couldn't even look them in the eye.

"He does sound like a good guy," Ken encouraged, and he squeezed my shoulder in an act of reassurance. If I had been looking up, I would have noticed that he winked ever so slightly to Mari. "I think we can find a person that could really help this *friend* of yours."

That was just one of multitudinous conversations I had with this man now sitting at the lunch table with the long, thin face, the gray closely-cropped beard, the half-framed reading glasses, and the flashing eyes of a Scotsman.

My eyes circled around the table over and over again and I silently thanked God for each and every man in attendance. A local man in an Aloha shirt, a man from Omaha who would fly all night to get to me, a man from Tacoma who can make sense of computers, a man from northern California with the perfect saddle shoes, a man from Boston in a *Strand* t-shirt and a Scotsman from the Bay Area—six of God's good gifts to me.

But I stated earlier there were ten others there and I've only told you about six. What about the other four? I could fill those four chairs with other dear friends like Lee or Bobby or Craig or Gary. They've all influenced me in big ways and small. They've all helped me in my life.

However, those weren't the names of the males that occupied those additional four seats. The remainder of the table was filled with four guys named Jesse, Jeffrey, John and Joseph.

My four sons.

They were 22, 19, 17 and 14 at the time. And they were all influenced big time by the other men surrounding them that Friday afternoon.

These six men meant the world to me and I wanted my boys to see it up close and personal.

\*　　　\*　　　\*

Returning again to the words of King Solomon, we see the value of other people in our lives:

*Where there is no guidance the people fall, But in abundance of counselors there is victory.*

—Proverbs 11:14 NASB

*A friend loves at all times.*

—Proverbs 17:17a NASB

The people we influence are affected, not only by us as an individual, but also by the people we bring to their lives. Family, friends, work associates, neighbors all create an influence. We can maximize this phenomenon by bringing the right kinds of people into this circle of everyday influence. That was the lesson my four sons learned that day.

I know I am an influence in the lives of my children, but I also know that they are influenced as well by the people I bring into their lives. That Friday afternoon in September was an opportunity for my sons to see six other men who have influenced me greatly in big and small ways. The influence of those men didn't end with me, but spilled over into the way I relate to my children.

Influence is everywhere. It even happens through the constellation of relationships where one person doesn't even know another person all that well, but the influence is there anyway.

The dictionary defines a 'companion' as 'a person who shares the experiences of another.' Those shared experiences get passed down the line and many others are influenced as a result.

**Influence multiplies through the lives of my friends.**

# CHAPTER 12

# The Celebration of Everyday Influence

celebrate

cel·e·brate

sĕl′ə-brāt′

VERB

1. To observe (a day or event) with ceremonies of respect, festivity, or rejoicing.
2. To perform (a religious ceremony).
3. To extol or praise.
4. To make widely known; display.

\*　　\*　　\*

A few years ago I was in Chicago giving the Keynote Address at a Business Conference. As is the well-worn routine, when I arrived at the Front Desk to check into the hotel, a packet of information was awaiting me. Beyond the typical fare from the hotel itself, this envelope contained all sorts of data about the weeklong conference that I would be kicking off. These types of conferences fascinate me with the variety of topics and the list of presenters, so once up in my room, I eagerly paged through the program to see what might be offered.

Jet lag brought on a small yawn as I paged through the program, observing business topic after business topic. But the program's last page was a clear departure from the normal listings. It announced an entire seminar track under the heading of *Personal and Family Development*. The offerings were much closer to home than *History of the Microchip, Actuarial Tables Update* or *Sales Tax and You,* so I grabbed a pen and circled the sessions that held the greatest personal interest.

The next morning, it was Keynote Speaker Uniform time, so I was dressed in my blue business suit with the faint, white chalk stripe, my powder blue French cuffed dress shirt, gold cufflinks, striped necktie in power red, and freshly shined black dress shoes. I grabbed my notes and made my way down the elevator to the Grand Ballroom for my presentation. It was still a little early for this group, so I did my best to warm them up with some humor and some extra energy before drilling down to my assigned topic for the morning, *Balancing Work and Life.*

In preparation for this speech, the Meeting Planner had stressed to me how busy these people are and how neglected the other areas of their lives can get. "Anything you could offer that would encourage us to be more balanced would be greatly appreciated," she virtually pleaded with me over the phone.

I told her I thought I could be of help and when the Keynote Session was ended that morning, it appeared that I had delivered on my promise. There was a hearty response, genuine laughter, including note taking and elbow jabbing. A splendid time was had by all.

After greeting a few people and shaking a few hands, a handsome man about my age, also dressed in the blue suited uniform of the day approached me with a toothy grin and an outstretched hand. We exchanged pleasantries and he was quite complimentary of my presentation.

"I'm doing a seminar that looks like it's going to be an extension of the remarks you made in the Keynote Address," he informed me. "We're going to meet in the Michigan Ballroom right after the morning coffee break. I'd love for you to sit in and let me know what you think."

I thanked him for cluing me in and told him I'd be delighted to slip in the back and join his session. After all, it was one of the sessions I had circled in my program, so I was more than willing to hear what he had to say.

The Coffee Break allowed for more handshaking, backslapping and business card swapping. Coffee ended up being optional, if you could somehow sneak a sip between power networking.

As I promised, I made my way to the Michigan Ballroom, sat discreetly in the back row and gave our presenter my undivided attention. He was good. He had insightful knowledge about his subject, coupled with a passion that was obvious. He had it all; stats, stories and slides. He even had some handouts with practical ideas for creating a deeper bond with those who are important to you.

I must confess, I don't remember a lot of the specifics of what he said, but what I do recall is a suggestion he made to those of us parents with adult sons and daughters who were already out of the house. He passed out a slip of paper that read as follows:

*Dear (Name of your son or daughter):*

*Looking back in your memory, what was the best day the two of us ever spent together? Try not to use an answer that involves anyone else—just you and me. If you can't decide between two or three, include them all. If you can't think of any, tell me that too.*

*Thanks.*

I was immediately struck by the nature of the assignment. He was inviting us to ask our kids to identify the best day the two of us ever had together. My head spun as I came to the disheartening realization that I could immediately answer that question as it related to my dad and me—it was the Thanksgiving with the Underwood typewriter, but I had no clue how any of my five kids would respond. Guilt poured over me like milk over cereal. I was drowning in a sea of shameful, soggy Special K.

Naturally, that handout ended up being an email that went out to all five of my adult children before the day's end. I couldn't get the question out of my mind. I frantically made valiant attempts to answer it on behalf of each of my kids. But I had little to no degree of confidence in any answer I created inside my head.

Before long, the responses from my children started arriving in my inbox. I was grateful they had all followed the directions correctly. Some listed more than one event, but each son or daughter referred to the top day that was spent together, just the two of us. Due to the nature of the assignment, each child's answer was different from the four others. Yet they were all the same in another way, a larger way.

Overwhelmed by their responses, my eyes welled up with tears of joyful recognition as I read their individual replies. By each email's conclusion I was weeping, unable to hold back the tears.

Just like I answered when asked to describe the best day I ever had with my Dad, all five of my kids had a response that could be generalized in the following manner:

*My best day with my Dad was the day he took me to work with him.*

Granted, the days we spent at work together involved far more exciting venues than the Freight Office on the banks of the Delaware. Some of the days they mentioned were actually exotic. But the emphasis in each of their notes was on the time we had together, just the two of us.

My daughter Joy referenced the time I took her with me on a Caribbean Cruise on which I was speaking. My son John pinpointed the trip to Hawaii we made together for me to deliver a speech to an arena full of educators. My son Joseph fondly recalled a trip that took us to the heart of San Francisco, staying in a very exclusive upscale hotel and enjoying the sights and sounds of the city.

But the number one answer was a trip to the International Platform Association in Washington D.C., given to each child individually during their summer vacations. My sons, Jesse and Jeffrey, both gave it the top slot in their best day recollections, and the other three all referred to it as number two.

It was none other than Daniel Webster, arguably the greatest orator of his time who founded the International Platform Association in 1831. An organization put together for public speakers, I first became acquainted with IPA in 1987 when I was beginning to create a strategy for launching a fulltime speaking career. A friend who was a member told me about their annual weeklong meeting, held every August in Washington, D. C. at the historic Mayflower Hotel. The format of the convention was to feature a cornucopia of speakers, all in thirty-minute time slots, providing exposure to the room full of people made up of potential clients, potential agents, meeting planners, speaker's bureaus, and fellow public speakers. My friend wisely counseled me to get as much exposure as I could before hanging out my shingle that I was available for speeches. "The name of the game is exposure," he said.

I hit the ground running that first week of August back in 1987. By week's end I accomplished my goal of 'getting exposure' and as a result was awarded The Hal Holbrook Award by the Association, which was given to the most promising up and coming speaker. It was sort of *American Idol* for speakers. They rewarded me with a lovely silver bowl and an even bigger reward—a thirty minute time slot in the final day's speaker's rotation.

I was given my place in the program. I would speak on Friday, right after media mogul Ted Turner and right before the head of the Central Intelligence Agency. It all becomes quite blurry after that, with the exception that I know I was received well and a few short months later I was out on my own, making a living as a fulltime public speaker.

IPA embraces their own and as a result of that positive first impression, I continued to attend the convention each August, where I continued to speak in their sessions and ultimately was invited to join their Board of Governors.

It was these August trips to DC that I began taking my kids with me, one by one, until they all had exposure to IPA by going to work with their Dad. Over those years of visits, my kids met people like Elizabeth Dole and Henry Heimlich and Jim Lovell and Steve Forbes. They've been with Cabinet members, Presidential hopefuls, Hollywood celebrities and military heroes. Yet all five kids maintain that it was the one on one time with their Dad that was the true highlight of the trip. Perhaps by recounting one of the trips with one of my sons, you'll better understand what it looked like:

Jesse, my oldest son, was up early the day we flew from California to the District of Columbia. "I couldn't sleep last night, Dad!" the eleven-year-old toe head exclaimed in excited tones. A dead ringer for his father, Jesse was doing his best not to arouse his three brothers and sister from their slumber. His mom had packed his child-sized suitcase with all the clothes he would need for a week's adventure together, yet she seemed to forget that this was two guys flying off together which was code for 'The Boy Is With His Dad, Meaning He Will Wear The Same Clothes All Week."

Wearing the same outfit all week was the least of his problems. That was the week Jesse got introduced to how his Dad eats while on the road. "We've got banquets every night that will serve a fine meal," I explained to him, as we were on our flight eastward. "As a result, I rarely eat anything during the day. Just coffee in the morning usually holds me fine until dinner. Are you going to be okay with that?"

"Sure, Dad," he boasted. "I'm with you."

We landed at Dulles, grabbed our luggage and hailed a cab. We were on Connecticut Avenue NW before we knew it. Once we were checked into our room, knowing we were subsisting on airplane peanuts and cokes, I suggested we visit the local McDonalds for dinner. Overjoyed, a huge smile broke out on my son's face, giving clear evidence that the boy was starving, just too polite to say anything to his Dad.

I had an early morning meeting the next morning so I let Jesse sleep in, promising him the night before I would come back up to the room at the 10 A.M. coffee break to make sure he was okay. I tiptoed out of our hotel room, chugged a morning coffee at the Coffee Shop, and instantly became fully engaged in the world of the IPA.

At precisely 10:00 A.M. I was in the elevator on my way up to check in on Jesse. Already awake, he was dressed in an outfit that looked surprisingly like the one he had worn all day yesterday on the airplane. Seeing that his suitcase was still unopened, my suspicion was confirmed.

"Dad.....," Jesse offered weakly.

"What is it?" I replied, sensing something was wrong.

"I hate to say this, but I'm kinda hungry."

Instinctively I glanced at my watch. Big mistake.

"I know it's still early," he apologized. "I guess I can wait till dinner. It'll be okay."

He said it with enough angst to make even the worst Dad feel compassion for the dying child sitting upright in the other unmade bed.

"I think we can rustle up some food, buddy," I said to him as I cracked open the Room Service Menu. A quick scan of the prices had me close the menu much faster than I opened it. Frantically I searched for a way to feed my starving child. "Hey, I know what we can do!" I volunteered with great enthusiasm. "There's a pharmacy just a block away. We can load up on some snacks for the room. How does that sound?"

Jesse nodded in complete agreement as the dawn of understanding arrived. When traveling with Dad, all normal food practices are suspended. Anything good for you will be reintroduced upon returning home to mother. For now, it's snacks and McDonalds. Now that's some special Father-Son bonding.

At the pharmacy, I was disappointed to find very little variety in the food section of the store. Fortunately they did have the staples that were part of every road trip I took back in those days—a bag of pretzels, a jar of peanuts and a six-pack of Diet Coke. Purchases made, let the feast begin!

As the evening banquet approached, Jesse was testing the waters to see if he could improvise on this eating plan. "Dad, did you say you were sitting at the head table tonight?" he asked that afternoon.

"That's right, son," I replied. "They usually put the Board members up front."

"Wellll . . ." he stammered, "I was wondering if maybe I could stay up here in the room and watch TV while you're at the banquet. Would that be okay?"

"What about dinner? Aren't you hungry?" I probed.

"Yeah, kinda," he replied. Suddenly his face brightened, as if he just that moment had an idea. "Hey, I know, we could get some McDonalds to go and I could eat it up in the room!" Of course this wasn't a spontaneous suggestion, but rather the careful planning of a young boy, plotting to eat fast food while watching hotel TV.

"Works for me," I responded, not wanting to spoil a trip that I was hoping would end up memorable. "I'll swing over to McDonalds right before I go to the banquet. Okay?"

"Great, Dad," Jesse answered with genuine gratitude. "You're the best!"

This eating schedule for the first full day of the convention ended up being the way it played out all week. For Jesse that meant pretzels, peanuts and Diet Coke all day, followed by a Big Mac, Fries and a Coke for dinner.

I thought the boy was loving it.

Ignorance is bliss.

The harsh light of reality hit with force about four days into our week. We were on the phone talking to the family back home. After I had a few minutes with each of Jesse's four siblings, his mom got on the phone. Politely, I let Jesse talk with her first. I couldn't hear what his mom was asking, but his answers left no doubt what the conversation was all about.

"Hi Mom! Yes I'm having a great time here with Dad." (pause) "He goes downstairs early every morning for meetings all day." (pause) "I go with him sometimes, but not all the time." (pause) "I stay in the room and watch TV." (pause) "No, Mom, I'm not watching anything I'm not supposed to." (pause) "Yes, I'm eating just fine, Mom." (pause) "Dad buys me McDonalds every night." (pause) "No, we don't do breakfast and lunch, Dad bought lots of really good snacks for us to eat here in the room."

It was at this point in the conversation I broke out in a cold sweat. The boy was telling the truth and in doing so, I was going to get busted by my wife. But I knew only half of the dilemma. I should have guessed something was up when at that point in the conversation, Jesse turned his entire body so that he was facing away from me as he began whispering on the phone to his mother.

"Mom, my stomach feels kinda yucky." (pause) "Yeah, I did. I barfed twice." (pause) "I do it while he is downstairs at the meeting so he doesn't really know what's going on." (pause) "No, Mom, I don't think we really want to tell him what's going on." (pause) "Okay, I will. I love you, too."

And with that he turned back to face me, thrusting the phone my direction and saying, "Mom wants to talk to you."

Placing the phone to my ear, I got a scolding that matched the one I got when I was a child and I ate an entire platter of shrimp, tails and all, at Captain Starn's Seafood Restaurant in Atlantic City. My mom was livid back on that day, just like my wife shared the same lava-like smoldering on this occasion.

Since we had been cooped up in the hotel all week, I decided the next day we needed a bit of a diversion. Finding a rental car establishment right there in the lobby of the Mayflower, I rented a compact car so Jesse and I could head out for a field trip. All my kids were very much into the U.S. Presidents, so I thought it would be perfect if Jesse and I took a drive down to Monticello, the home of Thomas Jefferson.

The Presidential comedy of errors began with me confusing Monticello with Mount Vernon. I thought Jefferson's home sat where Washington's home was located, so instead of a drive of just a few short minutes to the other side of the Potomac, Jesse and I had a journey of several hours through the hills and valleys of Virginia. Granted it was beautiful, but it must be remembered that this was in August so everything was looking just a little wilted in the super hot, super humid environment in the commonwealth known for its cute little jingle, *Virginia is for Lovers*. Forget it, lovers, it was too hot even for you that day. Come back in the fall for your lovin'.

Eventually we arrived in Charlottesville, the locale of Jefferson's home. Parking the rental car, we stepped out into the heat we had up to that point only seen, not felt. Instantly covered with sweat, our clothes stuck to our bodies like shrink wrap on ground chuck from the butcher. I made a mental note to suggest to Jesse that he may want to finally open his suitcase when we get back to the hotel.

We paid our admission fee and waited patiently for our tour guide to begin the tour. An old woman gathered our group together, announcing that she would be our guide that afternoon. Looking at her, she was unexplainably cool in temperatures that rivaled the sun. Besides her frigid ice-likeness, she had the appearance of being old enough to actually have known Jefferson personally. Wrinkles occupied the skin once reserved for makeup and hair that was formerly brunette was now steely gray. I wanted to make a joke of her age to Jesse, but fearing he would repeat it out loud, I kept my sarcasm to myself.

As we walked from room to room, it was immediately apparent that we had a heckler in our group. Every time we stopped to observe something of interest, this young woman would pipe up, "Didn't Jefferson sleep with one of his slaves and actually have children with her?" (This was back in the days before all these facts were confirmed, thus explaining the passionate questioning of our female Sherlock Holmes).

The guide responded with some innocuous generality about nothing being confirmed, so she would not comment on rumors. Visibly bothered by the young woman, the old woman pressed on. In the next room it started all over again. "Her name was Sally Hemmings. The slave girl. The one Jefferson slept with and had offspring." This time the tour guide responded even more harshly. "I will not dignify that comment with a response."

By the third room, a cool silence developed between the two ladies. The tour guide kept to her script while the young woman fumed in hot and humid silence. The temperature was debilitating and what would be a lovely excursion through American history became an endurance race against the elements. If he was so brilliant, why hadn't Jefferson thought to add air conditioning? If it was tough for an adult, it was brutal for an eleven year old.

Without malice or forethought, giving in to the power of the heat, Jesse wearily and innocently leaned on a piece of furniture in one of the later rooms on the tour. I don't know if it was an antique worth a million dollars, or if it was a belly full of heckling about Sally Hemmings, but either way, the tour guide went ballistic on my son. "Young man, we made it clear at the beginning of the tour that you are not allowed to touch anything. Please take your hands off that chair immediately or I will have you removed from the building!"

Jesse immediately obeyed. Looking my way, I could tell he was trying to ascertain whether he was in the same kind of trouble with me as he was with the tour guide. He wasn't. Frankly, I thought she overreacted, so as he looked my way, I rolled my eyes indicating my disbelief over what had just occurred. When we were a safe distance away from her, I whispered in Jesse's ear, "Don't let it bother you, Jess. She's having a bad day and she's taking it out on you."

His smile returned and we completed our tour of Monticello without further drama. I didn't give 'The Monticello Furniture Incident' much thought after that, but years later it would come back to me in a most meaningful way.

*       *       *

Part of the joy of supernatural influence is taking the time to reflect on exactly what God has done as a result of it. Natural influence should lead to supernatural influence and supernatural influence should lead to blessing in people's lives. The Scriptures consistently urge us to take time to remember what the Lord has done.

One of the definitions the dictionary gives the word 'celebration' is: 'to observe an occasion with appropriate ceremony or festivity.' When it comes to influence, I am choosing to, not only remember, but to festively observe that just as my best day with my father was the day he took me to work, so it is with each and every one of my children with their father as well. It's one of those full-circle sorts of experiences that is nothing short of supernatural. It's worth remembering and it's worth celebrating.

The Old Testament super-leader Moses understood the significance of celebrating.

> *For the Lord will pass through to smite the Egyptians; and when He sees the blood on the lintel and on the two doorposts, the Lord will pass over the door and will not allow the destroyer to come in to your houses to smite you. And you shall observe this event as an ordinance for you and your children forever. When you enter the land which the Lord will give you, as He has promised, you shall observe this rite. And when your children say to you, 'What does this rite mean to you?' you shall say, 'It is a Passover sacrifice to the Lord who passed over the houses of the sons of Israel in Egypt when He smote the Egyptians, but spared our homes.'"*
> —Exodus 12:23-27 NASB

The Passover Feast was a celebration of God's miracle of releasing the Israelites from Egyptian slavery. Every year, a feast, a celebration, a reminder of the supernatural influence from God Himself.

The trip to Washington was a wonderful one-on-one trip with my son, Jesse. I always thought it was a special time, but I'm not sure I would have ranked it as our best day. But he did and that's what matters. The day I sent out that email asking for the best day, he was the first of my five to respond. Here's what he said:

*What's the best day with you? The Washington D.C. Trip with you. The cokes, and pretzels and McDonalds, and puking, etc. Especially going to Monticello. I think the reason I really liked Monticello was because while we were on the tour I got tired and started leaning against the antique furniture and the tour guide yelled at me in front of everyone and told me that I was not to touch anything. I remember feeling really embarrassed and like I had just gotten in trouble and I remember looking up at you and you rolled your eyes and told me not to worry about it and that the lady was being really uptight. I loved that because it made me feel like no matter what, you were with me.*

That's a best day. In anybody's book. And nobody could have had that influence but me. Same goes for you—nobody can do this but *you*.

For my son, it wasn't about meeting famous people. Or eating fun food. Or a plane ride. Or hanging out, watching TV in a cool hotel.

*No matter what, you were with me.*

That phrase, best visualized by rolling my eyes in my son's presence had the same power as the four words '*you might like this*' had thirty years earlier.

Conversations of everyday influence.

Circumstances of everyday influence.

Celebrations of everyday influence.

**Influence is worth celebrating every day!**

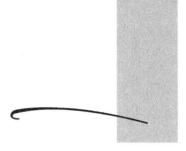

# Conclusion: The Culmination of Everyday Influence

culminate

cul·mi·nate

kŭl′mə-nāt′

NOUN

1. To reach the highest point or degree; climax.
2. To come to completion; end.
3. To bring to the point of greatest intensity or to completion; climax.

*    *    *

Some wonderful people have supernaturally influenced me in my life. Dad and Mom, Mr. Cassell, Miss Miller, Mrs. Heath, Mr. Doyle, Ron Von, Bart and Izzy, Prof and Chuck, Fred, Flan, Joe, Mike, Ron, Ed, Bob, Ken, my five kids and my dear wife, Kathi all come together for a fine list that is far from complete, but makes the point that influence can occur in both grand and minute expressions, but either way, it is every day. I am certain that I am a better man due to this everyday influence these men and women have passed along in my life.

However, there's a common misperception that a writer writes what the reader should do and he shares it confidently because he is already putting everything he's learned into practice.

Wrong.

Long before I began to create the outline for what would become this book, I knew full well that I had dropped the ball on many, if not all of the principles we have looked at so far. No role in my life was more suspect than my life as a father. My five kids were now grown and gone, raising families of their own and probably making the same mistakes, since most of what we know about parenting, we learn from our parents. That created deep heartache inside of me, but I did my best to offset those feelings with strong defense mechanisms.

I had what I thought was a long list of excuses—the best one being that we all experienced the trauma of divorce. These days I cringe as I think back on how totally empty I was in that season of grieving. I was beyond dysfunctional—I was non-functional. Impacting my kids in a positive way? Forget it. Influencing them in a supernatural way was replaced by a more basic goal—simple survival. As a painful illustration, well do I remember the summer evening I wandered into the kitchen unannounced, drawn there by an unusual aroma emanating from the microwave, only to discover my five children arguing in hushed tones so that I wouldn't hear their voices from my womblike recliner in the living room where they thought I was still permanently parked.

"I don't want to go in there and talk to him—you do it," one child said to another.

"No, I don't want to go in there either. You go talk to him."

"I don't know what to say to him. He's just so sad."

The look on their faces, when they discovered I was overhearing these words, can only be described as painful grief. Their dad was a mess, totally shut down emotionally; unaware of how unavailable he really was to those five souls that needed him the most. None of them could muster the energy to "minister" to me, thus nobody wanted to go into the living room and attempt to cheer me up. It was so sad, we should have huddled together and cried. But we were so emotionally devastated that we had no more tears left to shed. We had wept so much; all we had left was the crier's version of the dry heaves.

As difficult as that period of time was in our lives, somehow through God's grace, we were able to navigate the detoured highways. With the help of therapy, good friends, and God's good gift of time, perspective was regained and life went from reverse to neutral to forward. Our life's car was, once again, in D for drive and we were back making progress.

But, there was a pothole formed during that grieving process that was never even attempted to be re-filled. Much of what could have been communicated to my five during those all-important years of their youth had gone neglected. There was no stronger illustration of this gap than the spiritual aspect of their lives.

Being a man who made a large part of his living teaching spiritual truths from the Bible, one would think that my ability to teach these principles to my children at home would be second nature to me.

It wasn't.

Early on in my parenting life, I foolishly bought into the myth that my kids will learn spiritual truths from me by listening to me teach them in the formal, public speaking settings of my profession—in a church, or at a conference center, or a hotel ballroom. "I don't need to teach them at home," I rationalized to myself, "if they want it, all they have to do is pay attention at any of my presentations."

Yeah, like my kids were clamoring to sit on the front row every time I made a speech. I don't say that to denigrate my kids, because I have really good kids. But seriously now, what child given the choice to sit in a meeting with a bunch of adults or go outside and play with their friends would choose the former over the latter? Not many, and that included my tribe.

To make matters worse, I don't think any of this spiritual deficiency really occurred to me until about five years ago. Imagine, more than a decade went by without me even realizing that I had the opportunity to be a supernatural influence in the life of my kids, especially in the spiritual realm, and it never even crossed my mind! That is one sorry confession to have to make. Sad, but true.

Fast forward to 2010.

As I've already mentioned I had remarried in 1999 after seven years of being single again. My wife Kathi was remarkable on many fronts, not the least of which was to be a sounding board for my airing of problems for which she often offered solutions.

"I blew it with my kids when it comes to the spiritual side of their lives," I lamented to her one day while sitting together on the Family Room sofa. "I became my father—a man of few words—when I desperately needed to be talking." Lovingly, she encouraged me to vent more of my feelings of failure, hoping that if I flushed them from my system I wouldn't continue to dwell on them. But, she knew those issues had to be addressed and she offered me sage advice that changed everything.

"Do you remember when you wrote your book *The Promise of the Second Wind?*" she asked, giving me the impression she was changing subjects completely on me.

"Uh huh," I responded with virtually no energy.

"Good," she replied. "What was the subtitle of that book?"

"*It's Never Too Late to Pursue God's Best,*" I answered without thinking. Her eyes pierced into mine like fire and if I'm remembering it correctly, there was the slightest hint of a smile just peeking out of the corner of her mouth.

"Exactly," she said. "You are sad and disappointed that you missed so many opportunities to teach your kids spiritual truths—I understand your feelings of loss. But, Honey, you're not dead yet. You still have all sorts of ways you can impact your children, including spiritual impact. It's going to require that you get a little more creative, but you can do it."

"But they all live so far away now," I argued, tears starting to well up in my eyes. "Only one of the five lives even within an hour's drive. I can't . . . ."

"Stop right there," Kathi implored. "You talk to your kids just about every day, don't you? Between phone calls, emails and texts, you are in constant communication, right?"

"Yeah, I guess so," I replied, still in a daze of self-pity.

"And you're a smart guy," she continued. I hated to hear those words, because whenever she called me smart, it meant I was acting pretty dumb and needed to turn some things around. "Certainly you can figure out a way to connect with your kids so that you can become a more deliberate spiritual influence in their lives."

"I guess you're right," I conceded.

"Remember . . . *it's never too late.*"

With that, she squeezed my hand, gave me a kiss on the cheek and walked out of the room, leaving me alone with my thoughts. In a comic strip or animated movie, this is the part where the dynamite explodes above the guy's head in the dialogue bubble.

An idea was being born in my brain.

The first thing I did was check my bookshelf for the stack of daily devotional books I had collected over the years. Some were formatted as fifty-two readings (one a week), others included thirty-one readings (one per day for a month) and then I found the mother lode—a daily devotional with 365 readings (one every day for a full year). "Eureka, I have found it!" I said to the pile of dusty books sitting quietly before me.

On top of the pile was the devotional book that was the standard by which all other devotional books are measured. *My Utmost for His Highest* by Oswald Chambers has started the day for millions of Christians for close to a hundred years and it's as popular today as ever. As a testament to its popularity, I had multiple copies of the book, each in a different publication form. In the midst of hardbound copies, paperback copies, large print copies, slim line copies and leather-bound copies, I found exactly what I was looking for. It was a copy of the classic that included wide margins with lines on them, encouraging the reader to write his or her thoughts about the devotional each day. In a sense, it was more than a devotional, it was a journal. Quickly making note of the ISBN, I cranked up the almighty Internet and discovered that I could purchase multiple copies of this very edition through an online bookstore. Details typed in, I pressed 'Buy Now' and in a few days I was the proud owner of a box of *My Utmost for His Highest*, the Journal edition.

All this was happening mid-autumn of 2010, so I mapped out the next part of my plan that was scheduled to take place on Christmas of that year. When December 25th finally rolled around, all of us were together that year (a miracle all by itself) and under the tree, amongst a pile of presents for the grandkids, sat eleven gifts all of the same size and wrapped in identical paper.

When all the other gifts were distributed, I invited each of my five children, along with my three daughters-in-law, my son-in-law, my wife and myself to all open the final package at the same time. Wrapping paper removed, my kids sat staring at a journal version of *My Utmost for His Highest* that seemed to be staring right back at them from its position on their laps.

"I wrote you each a note that is in the front of the book," I volunteered, hoping to answer the questions each one indicated by the puzzled looks on their faces.

Each person received the same basic letter with a few personal modifications:

*Dear _____:*

*(First I would write a personal paragraph about something that occurred in the past twelve months that caused me to be proud of them)*

*I am choosing a Christmas present that I hope will assist us in staying better connected. Oswald Chambers (hitherto known as OC) is the classic devotional writer. Because it's an older work, he's not always easy to understand, but the extra effort will be worth it. I found this version that includes space for a journal entry of your personal thoughts. Not only can we read and reflect together, but think of this journal as a legacy you will leave to your children and the rest of the family.*

*I will send along an email every day with a summary of some of my thoughts as a result of reading the daily entry.*

*Kathi and I love you deeply and will continue to pray for you every day.*

*Love,*

*DAD*

The kids read the letter slowly. After processing it as best they could, some raised their heads and looked up right away. Others raised their heads and looked around the room, as if they were searching for a common soul with whom to commiserate. Still others didn't even lift their heads.

There was not a lot of excitement about this gift.

"I just feel like I dropped the ball in terms of giving you any spiritual direction," I blurted out to nobody in particular. "I thought this might be a way to make up a little for all that I neglected. This is not some forced assignment I am giving you. I'm hoping we'll enjoy going through it together. You can participate as much or as little as you'd like."

My words seemed to release some of the pent up pressure. Eventually all heads were up and smiles returned to the room. Some were genuine smiles, others fake smiles, all smiles trying to indicate they would be on board the best they knew how.

January 1st arrived a week later and I had my first opportunity to read OC and write an email to the family. First things first, however. I'm a bit of a nut about giving names to all manner of persons, places, things, and events in my life, so I knew I needed to do just that for this daily routine. Adoring acronyms like I do, I came up with the word BASE, which stands for Butterworth Active Spiritual Exercise. Each day in the subject column of the email, I would simply type in "BASE-01-01-11." (Obviously with the appropriate date each day).

It seemed stilted and forced to begin each email with some profound truth from OC, so I opted for a softer entrance and in doing so, I hit the jackpot. Instead of plowing into the devotional, I began each email with some softball newsy news that I thought might be relevant to the family. Sometimes it had to do with my travel, ("Greetings from Peoria! I spoke at a convention here last night and . . . ."). It could be a current event, ("There was a huge auto accident on the 405 freeway last night…"). Or it could be a personal memory, ("Twenty five years ago today I made a decision that ended up being far more significant than I ever imagined…"). If the date were a birthday or anniversary, I would begin the email with a bit of a tribute to the person or couple, ("Happy Birthday to Joseph! It seems like only yesterday you were playing T-ball and now you're a college graduate out on your own…"). And if all else failed, we could always discuss sports, ("Man, the Dodgers looked awesome last night, didn't' they? Do you think they can go all the way this year?").

Before that paragraph was finished, I would often write a sentence or two that would hopefully arouse some curiosity about the daily devotional, in hopes that they would read on.

After that paragraph of family stuff, I would get down to the nitty-gritty: a summary of the daily devotional and how it applied to me. Of course, that left open the possibility that it could also apply to each of them as well! On rare occasions, I would invite each of them to hit 'Reply All' and let us know what they were thinking. I say 'rare occasions' because I felt like that was adding too much pressure to this whole experience and again, what was really important was that I was communicating what I deemed to be relevant to my own life so my family could see the intersection of the spiritual and the actual. God makes a difference in my life every day and I finally had an outlet to make those important to me aware of that fact.

I'd love to be able to report that all of the family reads all of BASE all of the time. My guess is that would be a bold-faced lie. We have mixed responses among the eleven that participate. Some read my BASE email and the devotional every day. Others more sporadically. Some don't read the devotional, but read my BASE email every day. Still others are sporadic in that pattern as well. And then we have those who read the BASE email every day—but they only read the first paragraph! On occasion I can perhaps entice them to read a bit more then the opening, but they never miss the opening shot. You can decide if I'm making a difference in their lives or not, but I am choosing to believe I am at least doing more than I was doing prior to January 1, 2011.

We keep on keeping on. In 2012 we read together the daily devotional by Henry Blackaby based on his marvelous book, *Experiencing God*. In 2013, we enjoyed the daily words of the magnificent writer, Max Lucado. In 2014, I was able to find a daily devotional written by my former boss, Chuck Swindoll. His *Day by Day* was especially meaningful to us, since we knew this author in a more personal way. In 2015 we are learning much from our friend David Jeremiah, in his daily work entitled *Discovery.*

\*      \*      \*

There's nothing sacred about reading a daily devotional and then emailing those you want to impact. All I'm trying to do is motivate you to embrace the spiritual side of your influence on others. It doesn't matter if you read them a book, show them a movie, download a video off the Internet or take them all to Israel for a month. You can and must teach spiritual concepts to those around you. Get inventive. It can happen and you can do it.

The Apostle Paul encouraged the Philippian believers with this thought:

> *For I am confident of this very thing, that He who began a good work in you will perfect it until the day of Christ Jesus.*
> —Philippians 1:6 NASB

God is not finished with you yet. It doesn't matter how old you are or how young you are. How sick you are or how healthy you are. What a success you've made of your life or what a failure it has been. None of that matters. It's never too late to pursue God's best.

So remember the bottom line: you can do whatever you want to do in order to impact those around you with supernatural influence. And for those of us who think we missed our opportunity, allow me to state it one more time . . .

**_Influence . . . it's never too late._**

# About the Author

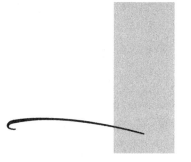

**Bill Butterworth**'s extraordinary ability to blend humor, story-telling, wisdom and practicality has made him one of the most sought after communicators in venues throughout North America. Through his wit, warmth, insight, and realism, he brings help and hope to his audiences everywhere.

Bill holds a Bachelor's degree from Florida Bible College and Masters' degrees from both Dallas Theological Seminary, and Florida Atlantic University. He was on the faculty of Florida Bible College for eight years and he was Director of Counseling Ministries at Insight for Living, the radio ministry of Chuck Swindoll for seven years. Bill now devotes himself full time to encouraging people through speaking, writing and ghostwriting. Because of his remarkable abilities, Bill was awarded *The Hal Holbrook Award* by the International Platform Association, naming him one of the select few to be named a Top Rated Speaker.

Since 1988, Bill has traveled full time speaking to hundreds of audiences as small as 18 and as large as 18,000. Not only has he been warmly received at such great churches as *Willow Creek Community Church* and *Saddleback Community Church*, his *Fortune 500* clients include Microsoft, Walt Disney, Ford, Chrysler, Bank of America, and Verizon. Plus, Bill has addressed 26 teams in the National Football

League, as well as over a dozen teams in Major League Baseball and the National Basketball Association.

In 2004, Bill established the *Butterworth Communicators Institute* to train men and women to find their speaking voice and raise their speaking ability to the next level. The overwhelmingly positive response to BCI has been gratifying as students maximize their skills through this intensive, yet intimate three-day workshop.

In the writing world, Bill has authored over a dozen books under his own name and more than two-dozen as a ghostwriter. He believes that every story is worth sharing and relishes the opportunity to help others get their story in print.

For more information on Bill, please visit his website at www.BillButterworth.com

**BILL BUTTERWORTH**
**www.BillButterworth.com**

# CONTACT INFORMATION

To order additional copies of this book, please visit
www.redemption-press.com.
Also available on Amazon.com and BarnesandNoble.com
Or by calling toll free 1-844-2REDEEM.

CPSIA information can be obtained at www.ICGtesting.com
Printed in the USA
BVOW08s0321150515

400496BV00003B/3/P